My Past Lives and How They Came Back to Haunt Me

❖

By Acacia Lawson

Copyright © Acacia Lawson, 2021

Cover design: Katie Lee Burns @of_our_ancestors

Editor: Alex Pop @AlexPopWriter

Interior design: Acacia Lawson

All rights reserved. This book or parts thereof may not be reproduced in any form, stored in any retrieval system, or transmitted in any form by any means—electronic, mechanical, photocopy, recording, or otherwise—without prior written permission of the author, except as provided by United States of America copyright law.

For permission requests, write to the author, at www.byacacia.com.

The information given in this book should not be treated as a substitute for professional medical advice; always consult a medical practitioner. Any use of the information in this book is at the reader's discretion and risk. The author cannot be held responsible for any loss, claim, or damage arising out of the use, or misuse, of the suggestions made, the failure to take medical advice or for any material on third-party websites, books or movies.

For my mother –

My most exquisite friend and confidante.
My cheerleader and ally.
Thank you for having me.

And my love –

You are my person, my soulmate and my partner.
I am so happy to co-create with you.
Thank you for being my king.

Introduction

❖

This book name and idea came to me while I was lying on my yoga mat in Bali, trying to relax into corpse pose after a hard yoga session that I had pushed my body into.

My past lives have revealed themselves to me slowly throughout the past 5 years, as if to let my human brain come to the conclusion that I was not completely insane, and that these very real visions were imprinted on my energetic soul blueprint, waiting to be exposed as the innate and outdated relationship patterns I seemed to repeat in this lifetime along with the unconquered, irrational fears that tended to immobilize me at odd and inconvenient times throughout my life.

At first, I did not want to write a book such as this. I rather imagined my first book to be one of great spiritual enlightenment, or at least a step by step self-help book with examples from my own healing process.

After much debate within myself regarding past lives, what reality is, and the purpose of this book, along with everything else going on in the world right now, I hope these chapters can help you in discovering who you truly are and what your soul has come here for, this time around.

In my past life regression channeling, I see the last 24 hours of life, and the frenzied moments leading up to my death, accented by moments of victory, sex, royal intrigues, and every-day problems. Through different time periods, I process my mindset during those last 24 hours.

These chapters are in no particular order, and were written in streams of consciousness. The words are in current day American English for ease of reading and interpretation. I have had more than ten past lives, but these are the lives that wanted to be depicted in this book per the streams of consciousness.

If there's anything I've learned, it's that the soul will scream to be heard or it will shut down completely; killing the human vessel it is in currently, in order to come back again (reincarnate) birthed into another human body until the lessons are learned. This reincarnation is how a person can experience déjà vu and other seemingly 'supernatural' occurrences.

One way or another, our energies must be examined and it is our duty, as humans, to become one with our higher self so that we live our most amazingly brilliant life in love and abundance – the life we have only dreamt of living before we die; instead of waiting for the next life to fulfil our dreams, or some pipe dream about spending an eternity (if you're a good kid and not denied entrance) walking around some heaven in the clouds.

We are creating heaven on earth by examining our lives and past lives, and living our current life to our fullest, happiest self. Your reality exists inside of you; 'as within, so without'. Have the courage to go forth, grab those dreams with both hands, and make them happen.

I hope that you enjoy the journey you are about to step into by reading this book. It's full of everything that makes up a human life (or ten) and so much more.

Your friend on this journey,
Acacia

My Past Lives and How They Came Back to Haunt Me

❖

Contents

Introduction	5
Chapter 1 *The Tibetan Monk*	11
Chapter 2 *The Druid Priestess*	33
Chapter 3 *The Mongolian Warlord*	61
Chapter 4 *Queen Elizabeth's Court*	83
Chapter 5 *Native American Daughter*	105
Chapter 6 *The Viking King*	127
Chapter 7 *The Hunted Wife*	157
Chapter 8 *The Village Healer*	181
Chapter 9 *The Glory of Rome!*	201
Chapter 10 *Versailles*	227
Chapter 11 *The Afterword*	245
About the Author	257

Chapter 1

The Tibetan Monk

❖

487 CE

Most ancient written records of Tibet were destroyed by the surrounding raiding countries, angry kings and religious land grabs. Bön and Buddhism were widely practiced together, and holy places were revered despite the tumultuous Tibetan landscape and fractured society.

There was no way I could do it again. I was getting too old for this world. I was no young monk in training. I would not leave my home this time.

I had been alive for one hundred and eighty-five years. I had seen the rise and fall of different lords and lands.

All of the wise seekers from other languages and religions that had come to learn from me. I witnessed the failure of one religion after another. The decline of sacred energy practices and knowledge. I had hoped that the few I had shared my knowledge with would take it back to their lands and create a whole new society.

But we had heard no such news; in fact, mainly death, destruction, and the never ending war for power was the only news that trickled through for the past one hundred years.

I had prayed for more peace and love. I had spent my life in the service of others. I had learned so much and shared so much. I had forsaken my family for this inner quest of serenity.

I could move the energy out of people and activate them into their true selves. I could design a whole new way of being for a person just by sitting in the same room with them for two minutes.

Most of my time was spent removing the fear from the bodies of children. There was so much terror and death. Constant feuding and taking of lands. An exchange of lives for monies and other things that could not go with you when your body died.

We had no need for continued generations trapped in fear. We needed more love and compassion, not beings trapped in the eternal energy consuming death of the soul, also known as fear.

To remove the fear from children, I would go to the astral plane where I was needed the most. Children held captive or in isolation, wounded or abused, women in childbirth, people dying for unnecessary reasons. These were the ones I would search out in my meditative state and try to help.

First, I would protect my body and energy with intense prayers and rituals and then start the dream state. Once I was on that energetic plane, my energy went immediately to the ill, scared or dying. Then I would take their fear energy and release it, cleansed into a neutral energy, back into the universe. I replaced their fear with joy and love.

Most would end up weeping and no longer be scared. Some would fight it energetically; those were the ones that I would let fall asleep before going in again. Then I would find their energy and fix it without their conscious mind fighting back.

There was so much death in this world already. So much fear orchestrated by men and wars, and getting too far away from what we simply are, spiritual beings. There is no way that this current world could ever be the utopia from whence it originated.

Somewhere along the way, greed had taken hold. The intense power struggle for control and domination over all humans, and all other beings, had given rise to a powerful few in every part of the world.

These powerful few readily embraced the dark side in their perpetual search for more.

Most people have no idea this struggle exists. They think they are simply put here to live their lives, have their kids, do their work and then die. They don't question, they don't break from the crowd, nor ever seek the truth.

These people are easier to manipulate and most are manipulated from a young age. Even with a belief system in place, three quarters of them are scared of death and will listen when the ruling authorities instruct them to do anything. The stricter the laws are, the more people believe they are safe from death and destruction. Obey your master!

Would it always be this way?

When so much could be achieved if people would activate their souls...it was sad to me. At some point, we had gotten away from the deep soul-knowledge, the beliefs that held people to a higher plane of consciousness and a more enriched experience, not only existing or simply getting by.

Now these higher consciousness rituals were for a few brave souls, and most of them tried to spread it to others. Hopefully, the reconnection of oneness with the god source would lead them to ways which had been lost; which would be rediscovered and practiced so that everyone could experience energetic freedom.

The story often repeated within our walls, once a monk had reached a certain level, was when the healer called Yeshua had come to stay with us. All of the monks who were present had been surprised. He came to learn all that the masters could teach him and he was a quick learner. He had been with the Druids in Ireland for some time before he landed here and even studied with the ancients in India.

He shared a lot of that knowledge with our elder masters, along with his Egyptian energy rituals. They had learned so much from him and he was a great, compassionate spirit.

But even he could not fight the evil completely. It was too large; it seemed like every year it grew, more silent and deadly than the previous year. There were only so many of us fighting against this evil in any way that we could.

I digress... This is what happens with age, lots of digressing.

My days consist of praying for five hours and then healing people for five hours. I have one meal a day since that is really all the body needs, and mainly it consists of nuts and vegetables. Sometimes fruit. I only need five hours of sleep each night.

Much of my time is spent around the animals of the monastery. They are such loving creatures.

Another fun exercise is writing down my learnings and theories. Reading and making corrections, rewriting and enjoying what I have written.

The seekers who come after me will have all the knowledge they need from my books and writings. My hope is that they, too, will pass this knowledge down to others.

However, we learned how the Essenes were wiped out and scattered in the wind. All of their knowledge, their libraries, their teachers, their energy masters, gone. Lost awareness, energy and wisdom.

It had happened multiple times, before and after, in different civilizations. Similar to Atlantis.

Once the spiritual masters get too close in helping people transition to embody pure love by acceptance of their energetic forms in order to create a true heaven on earth, evil creeps in and destroys the entire civilization. Then the people start rebuilding, from nothing, based on their feelings but not entirely sure of themselves.

Due to this cyclical destruction, not only of cultures and places but also of written knowledge and steps towards the enlightened way, I have become more careful in what I write and how I write it. I make copies of everything and hide them in a place outside of our walls. As much as I know our energy protects this sacred ground, there is no telling when some powerful person would decide that we have outlived our usefulness.

There would be entire days that I would not speak with anyone inside of these walls. Sometimes, I would purposefully go entire weeks hiding from my brothers and speaking only to the animals and god.

My higher self, my intuition, led me to take certain actions. I had let it lead me since childhood. I always wondered if my true self had been strong in my past lives, since I have clearly let it direct me in this life.

~~~

I have no regrets over this path I have taken. My karma is clean.

Glancing around my tiny room, I knew that there was no place I would rather be.

"Brother Jalus, we must hurry. We have had the news. Three sanctuaries have been burned to the ground. Gather what you can of your writings and we will move them from here," one of my fellow monks claimed, rushing into my room.

"Are the marauders headed this way?" I asked.

What did it matter? The time had come.

"We have no idea. The messenger that brought us this news said that all towns around us are surrendering to their leader and that no one is resisting. And yet they still burn down our holy places," he replied mournfully before quietly departing.

That was not a good sign. Another fiend bent on destroying more wisdom and enlightenment. Yet I had known this day would come.

If all scholarly men of every religion would come together and decide that peace and love would rule the world, and ensure that those teachings would spread in their communities, there would be no more killing. No more greed. No more need for these power-hungry heathens to perpetually destroy what they could not tolerate; energetic and soul freedom. True freedom on this planet and in this life.

I rushed around my cell-like room, stuffing books and journals into bags. Getting everything I could into them without damaging the books.

Three monks appeared at my doorway.

"We will take the bags that you have ready, Brother Jalus. We head to the south. Towards India," one said.

"Towards the south you will most likely encounter hostiles and more problems. The north is safer," I replied.

"The north would kill us all. It is inhospitable land, especially with the cold setting in. However, there is a safe community in northern India for us to continue our work," said another.

"Thank you, brother." I pointed at the seven bags of books on the bed. "These are ready."

Two of the monks struggled under the weight of the bags. The heavy-set monk did not.

Scuffling to the door of my room, the heavier monk looked back at me and said solemnly, "You should leave soon, Jalus. I have felt, and looked deeply into, the energy heading this way. It is very vicious and dark."

Nodding at him, I quietly chided him, "It is our duty to heal and help. Perhaps my path was meant to cross this formidable leader and bring him back to god. Or he is to be my death. Either way, it does not matter. I am old and I will not last the length of the journey. I appreciate your care and providing the transport of my books. May they guide all of the future generations of our sect."

His face remained grave as he quickly bowed and hastened away.

With their leaving, the hallways became silent. Every monk had departed for India.

There was a feeling of calm before the storm; as if all of my life had been leading up to these hours or days before the wrathful brigands would arrive.

I will keep praying. There is no need to transfer any worry to the animals.

As I got down on my knees, I felt the presence of many guides before me. It was an insular experience, allowing me the feeling of protection and comfort.

"Please protect all of the beings within these walls. Even the animals deserve to die without fear," I murmured to the heavens.

My mind wandered.

What would I miss the most when I leave this body? I made a small mental list.

1. Petting the animals lovingly and running my fingers through their soft hair,

2. The sweet taste of our dried fruits. I wonder if there were any that had been left behind in the kitchen?
3. How the sunset danced around the mountains, as if it might stay for a few more hours, making me think the sun was not on a particular course at all,
4. The heavy smell of incense burning before prayers,
5. And the beautiful, somewhat mournful, sounds of our prayers that were sung in a heavy harmony that echoed up towards the heavens.

This list is where I would start because evil was flying rapidly towards this place. I could feel their anger and hatred, obstinate with the desire to kill and destroy everything.

The animals gathered around me as I slowly made my way to each of them. I whispered words of love and encouragement as I touched each one and looked into their eyes.

Their souls were so scared. They too could feel the negatively dense vibrations being sent through the earth and into the air. I had nothing to assure them with but I removed as much of their fear as I could.

Each one of my healing gifts was lessening as my energy was draining slowly from my body. My time was coming.

"It would be merciful, my beautiful soul, if you would leave this body before it is hacked to pieces by these bandits," I joked to myself.

Humor always made these earthly situations seem less important. After all, I was headed to my soul's home and there was no better feeling than the peace of knowing what I knew awaited my soul's departure from this body.

The animals eyed me suspiciously when I did not make them go to their cages and pens for the evening. I even left the front gate open for them to leave, if they chose.

Who was I to demand they face a potential death march with me? I was not an Egyptian, I thought, and I laughed some more.

I made my way to the kitchen and searched for the dried fruits. I found a few apricots and cashews. There was no cheese left, but this was still a feast.

Savoring every morsel, I thought of nothing. I cleared my mind to enjoy the gritty texture of the sweet apricots and the buttery velvetiness of the cashews. I deliberated on where the apricots and cashews came from; what merchant or tradesman had brought them to us, I speculated as I continued chewing thoughtfully.

~~~

Sunset would happen soon. My final sunset on this abandoned mountain. The small town had cleared out hours ago and most inhabitants would likely never return to their homes.

Climbing the stairs to the upper level of the watchtower, I counted every step, knowing that this would be my final trip to see the miraculous view. The magic contained in sunrises and sunsets can make even the least spiritual person feel peace and serenity, until the spell is broken by their disjointed mind, prodding them to get back to work and to feel nothing in their numbed existence.

If only there was a way to bottle the energy of sunsets and hand it out to the masses, returning them to their souls, back to god source.

The orange ball of the setting sun started to touch the mountain tops, painting the valley with a hazy, warm glow. Pinks and purples danced across the sky while the clouds whispered trails of white; lazily weaving their way on the top and to the sides of the sun.

If this is not heaven, I do not know what is, I reflected.

How could such perfection be overlooked daily by most people? This was the artistic masterpiece of Earth, the offering of solace and contentment to the most weary of people. Perhaps one day, viewing a sunrise or sunset would become a daily habit amongst all nations. One could hope and dream...

As the sun sank behind the mountain ridge, somberness filled the air. Tonight would be melancholy for this old monastery. Energy is left behind in many sacred areas and buildings, especially if those buildings have remained intact for hundreds of years.

Walking slowly down the steps, I turned toward the prayer room. I lit the incense and walked around, wafting the pungent smell into every corner of the room.

Once cloaked in the aroma, I lifted my voice to the heavens and sang a prayer that I had learned when I first arrived to commence my monkhood.

"The blessings we receive are gifted to us through our faith and acceptance of your will. We are the truth and we speak the truth. Let all who enter and all who pray, never forget from whence they came."

One of the dogs started to howl, a sorrowful sound against the silence of the dusk. They were on their own now. I could do nothing more for any of the animals and they could feel it.

Thoughts started to come to me, circling around my head; ideas of how my life could have gone and how easy my life had been in the home of my father.

I was to follow in his tradesman footsteps and marry a fellow tradesman's daughter, combining their businesses creating greater wealth. I would have been a fat, married grandfather or great-grandfather by now. Instead, I had run off at the guidance of my higher self. My mother had named me Jalus, which means rainbow body; what did they expect with such an energetically prophetic name?

I had devoted myself to this life of service, energy healing and prayer. Whereas many people went hungry, I was always provided for with a roof over my head and a belly full of food and sustenance. Except for the days or weeks I chose to fast.

Thank god, I will never have to fast in this body again, I smiled. Fasting helped with total control over the body and mind, and also cleansed the body of impurities and disease. It was hell on earth for many until the body became adapted to it.

We are but souls having a human experience. The body can either master the soul, or the soul can master the body and thus the mind. Many people cannot fathom this type of wisdom, this innate knowing, and instead struggle from day to day, wallowing in grief, anger, jealousy and self-pity.

My life held none of those limiting, base emotions. I wondered if it ever had in a previous life… I must have been good in my past life to deserve this life, for my lessons during this lifetime were not a hardship. Most humans regard monks with awe, yet at the same time have an incorrect assumption of monks being limited in this life…as if we lack in something by living a cloistered, minimal existence!

There had never been a time in my life where I wanted to be anywhere else but in service to god, to humankind and to my writing. I was beyond blessed.

Yet my human experience this time was coming to an end. There was a liberating feeling emanating from my body. My energy knowing it would soon return to unite with source, to the love and peace that it belongs to.

For as much as our bodies love to feel, taste, smell, hear and see, (those experiences are imprinted upon our souls), our bodies do not want to die. They want to live forever. And our minds try to convince us that this can be possible, if certain measures are taken.

So instead of living life to the fullest, reveling in each miraculous moment, our minds are constantly searching for the magic elixir, the spell that would keep us here, whatever needs to be done to draw this time out.

That is where it goes wrong for so many. They become stuck in that loop. Reliving a pattern or pain-point, refusing to change, stating that this is how they had always done it. There is no yielding, no desire to relearn, or to try a different way.

Oh, the endless bargaining our minds will do to make us fall under its spell...

Many choose the dark path. The devil's way, as some call it. The rise by means of black magic, which also can be called selling one's soul to the devil. Satan. Lucifer. The Dark Side. The Maker of the Unspoken Realms. The Stealer of Souls. Dark Energy Harvesters. The Reptilian Race. There are many names for it.

Once a person made the agreement and called in that dark energy, there was no going back. Not in this lifetime. And those around the person were not safe. Their children and families would come under this darkness as well.

I had tried to help families break free of this generational bondage. Some families I was able to help, but many individuals had given in. Their eyes would appear mostly black, the color (and the life) gone from them; replaced with a feverish look of never-ending greed, a desire for possessions, and a deep hunger for more.

That was always a strange experience; when someone would come to me with the black eyes, their family carrying them to me despite their bodily struggle. I would examine the person and feel the extent of the darkness while they were tied to a chair. If it had reached approximately over the sixty percent mark, there was nothing I could do, for my energy was not as strong as the Ascended Masters. Even with the energetic contribution from my brothers used in the ancient rituals, more than our combined energy was needed to remove the energetic soul contracts and oaths that floated in the other dimensions.

Many of these poor souls had escaped from their families and gone on to wreak havoc on anyone in their path. They would lie, murder and steal, and somehow rise ever higher within the ranks of certain lords or become a lord themselves.

In order to protect our humble walls, we had to think of the masses we had helped in the past and would help in the future, and not the handful of evil ones that darkened our doorstep every ten or so years.

But how did you know if you made the right choice? What if I was supposed to release their energy from their body, from this plane, so that no harm would come to those in their path? This meant to kill their body and release their soul.

There was guidance, of course, from god. However, when stories would reach us about the few that we had not tried to help and the butchering they left in their wake, doubt would come into my mind as to whether we had made the correct decision.

Had we done more harm than good?

Of course, this is why I was not in charge of this hermitage. That type of leadership was not in my realm. I preferred my writings and teachings, not to coddle a bunch of grown men into believing in themselves and their gifts.

I shook my head and stood up, my knees creaking as I rose. All of this pondering. Where had the time gone?

Exiting the prayer room, I saw that it was completely dark.

Would I sleep this night? Or listen and wait? It would be my last sleep in this body. What a joy to know that my soul was soon to be released.

This earthly body was wearing out.

I made my way to my room and fell upon my small bed.

"Thank you, god," I whispered as my breathing slowed and my body relaxed into the peaceful slumber of a soul that knows complete tranquility.

~~~

I woke up with a start.

There had been a crashing sound that reverberated throughout the building. The bandits must be here.

Slowly, I got up and began to walk down the hall. I could feel the heavy energy; the energy of destruction, darkness and despair. It made me frown. These men needed more help than all of the people I had served over the last one hundred years.

This would be interesting. I don't think I had brushed this closely with deeply ingrained evil - ever. What lesson was I to learn today that would carry over into my future life?

Or was this experience, and my part in it, simply a lesson for one of them?

For the outcome would be but one: my death. I had felt it and foreseen it. There was no running.

Coming to a halt in the courtyard, I surveyed the damage. Everything was in chaos, all of the animals gone and all of the bins and baskets turned over, which wasn't very smart. Food and water were not exactly flowing plentifully in this area of the world. It was a hard land.

Apparently, they were not very smart. I stifled a wry laugh. Here was a wrinkle in their tough warrior role.

Where was the leader? My eyes danced from man to man, trying to discern which dirty warrior was in charge.

A man marched up to me, grabbing me by the arm and swinging me this way and that as he yelled into my face, "Where is all of the gold, the food, the monks, everything?"

"Not here. There is some food in the kitchen," I responded calmly.

He screamed, "There is nothing but dried fruit in the kitchen!"

His face became mottled, as if he could not draw in a complete breath, and he loosened his hold on me, allowing me to escape his harsh grip and step backwards... right into a very hard, unyielding, much taller man.

"Alright, old man. Where is everything?" the tall man questioned me softly.

I turned around and glanced up at his face; he was familiar.

I drew in a sharp breath. "We have met before. I feel it in your energy," I whispered to him.

"Oh yes, we have met. Many years ago. Where is the gold and the books of wisdom?" he asked.

"You came here to exact some type of revenge, didn't you?" I questioned him.

He shrugged before answering, staring over my head at something off in the distance. "Of sorts. You banished me from playing with the children in the village square. We were all beggars but you said I was teaching them bad habits and skills. You lorded over me, saying that I was leading them towards the dark and they were meant for the light. When you banished me, all of the townspeople refused to help me. I was refused food as a child! Do you know what that did to me?"

"I can imagine," I gently replied.

"Oh, imagine all you want to, old man. But you will never know the hell I went through. The pain I suffered because of your self-righteous piousness. The humiliations and battles I've gone through. And I vowed in my teen years that I would come back here and settle the score. Burn you to the ground because I knew you would still be alive. Someone as horrible as you could never die a natural death. That is why I am back. To send you swiftly to your death so you cannot injure any more people as you hurt me."

I nodded.

It had all come flooding back as he spoke. I could feel the young children and how they looked up to me. I was in my early forties and had come into my energetic gifts and knowledge completely. These children had listened to my words and many of them later became gifted monks. Some moved away, searching for a better climate and mates with whom to make families with.

Back then as small children, they had needed my guidance.

He had been such a wicked child. His parents had abandoned him at the age of four, his mother stating he had the devil in him after he brutally and mercilessly cut off the heads of all of their chickens. Perhaps she had cursed him. His father had three other sons and leaving one behind meant nothing to him, especially one that was so troubling. His family never returned to this region.

When I say he was a wicked child, I don't mean a naughty boy as all children can be. He would steal anything and everything and never repent for it. Somewhere he had either learned or inherently knew how to kill animals slowly and watched them suffer with a smile on his face. Five children had witnessed this on different occasions until finally one of the adults had followed him to see if it was true. He saw this boy tie up a dog and dismember it slowly and then drink some of its blood while grinning like someone in the clutches of insanity.

My decision to expel him from our small town was in order to save the others. I knew that I had made the right choice.

That would mean this man was over one hundred years old as well. Well! This was highly unusual. Most people did not live that long unless they were energy healers.

"Little did you know that your exile would turn me into the sorcerer I am today," he continued.

I stared at him. Feeling into his energy, I could sense the deep, dark coils feasting on his soul energy. In fact, his eyes were as black as a fathomless pit.

"Listen monk, we all know how this will work. You will die and I will carry on, searching for children and gold, as is my mission," he nonchalantly said, one corner of his mouth twisting upwards into a smirk. "I was hoping your books would lead me to the energy secrets I did not learn from my master. But you are smarter than you look. You knew I was coming, did you not?"

I nodded. The less I spoke, the more quickly this would go.

"You are so much smaller than I remember, yet you had put so much fear into me back then. I spent years loathing you. Cursing you. Waiting for news that you had died. Every traveler that came my way would talk of your healings, your wealth of wisdom, knowledge, and your compassion. Where was that compassion towards a small boy who could barely fend for himself? What made me the worst? You condemned me after my parents had rejected me. How was I ever to recover from that?" he pondered aloud as he scanned the courtyard.

He had obviously been asking himself these questions for many years.

"We do not need your food, monk. We need nothing from you but your death. The world will rejoice once you are gone from it," he proclaimed victoriously.

As if killing me would be the end of his troubles...

I sighed and shook my head, staring at the ground, hoping he would get on with it quickly.

"Oh, I see. You think you don't have to answer me because you are going to die? Wrong, monk. I will keep you stretched out alive and slowly bleed you to death until you answer me!"

He started towards me with his long legs consuming the space between us. I was not scared and showed no fear, but I could see that he was trying to intimidate me. I had faced much worse than him in my energetic healings. As much dark magic as he had learned, he was still only a man.

Horror stories are for scaring small children from doing bad. They have no effect on me.

This man was trying his best to be the ultimate evil. It seems as though he missed the mark. He had not gotten all of the information he needed to take the final dark step. Thank god I had hidden the books. He would corrupt their teachings and twist them for his own gain.

"I will not apologize for my decree when you were a child. You were, and are, an evil little boy. You think you can kill on a whim, that every living being is nothing but an insect under your heel to be stamped upon as you see fit. That is where your soul was and always has been. I care not what you do to me now. My life has been long enough."

"Oh, how noble you are, monk. Why, one would think that you had royal blood. I never did know your birth or from whence you came. I wonder if that was in your beloved books?"

I glanced at him. 'I wonder if I could energetically remove any of the darkness inside of him,' I pondered.

"No, monk. You cannot remove my energy or heal me or whatever you call it. But I can remove yours," he laughed.

Looking down, I could feel my chest squeeze tight, the air in my lungs leaving suddenly. So, this was how he would kill me?

"Not yet, monk. Not yet," he said from behind me. "One last question. If I were to go into your mind, would I find where you have hidden the books? I do love to play games."

Now! It was time to leave my body. I had prepared for this my entire life, knowing that I could choose when to leave if I so wanted. This was not so much a choice, but a necessity. He must never have the books.

"Ah, ah, ah. Not so fast, monk. I know what you are capable of. I will not let you leave your body until you have answered my questions."

He was not even close to me. I had to admit that his power was greater than I had anticipated, almost greater than my own gifts. But, I had studied the books and I understood where his power came from. How to get his darkness away from my soul, so that it would not follow me into the next life; this was my final act.

As he closed his eyes, seeking entry into my mind, believing in his ability to gain the information he sought, I understood what the book on dark magic had warned of. Power held by this one man could be a threat, not only to humankind, but to the entire earth and planetary system.

Keeping my eyes on him while blocking his access to my mind, I focused on my breath and the energy I called forth in my reserves and from my god source. Sealing in my energy, I sent it back up to the heavens.

His wild eyes flew open and his face contorted with rage. "No!" he shouted, as he raced towards me.

He grabbed my arms to keep my body upright in a vain attempt to keep me alive, but it was too late. I had passed the threshold.

"You cannot live forever. Your time is soon," I murmured to him as my soul started to leave my body. I inherently knew what was coming.

"You lie! You have been and always will be a liar!" he was screaming at my body as he pounded it with his fists; yelling and raging, blood flying everywhere, his men looking at anything but his maddened rage mutilating my body.

Floating above my dead body, I realized that I too had once been this dark of a man in a previous life and that this current life is where I learned about the fine balance of good and evil that hung perilously upon this world and within me.

The balance between the light and the dark; the thing of nightmares and stories from long ago. The battles that raged between heaven and hell, the good and the bad, the righteous and the fallen; those conflicts aren't in some faraway place in the sky or in some other world beneath our feet.

They are here, on this earth, in us all, in every lifetime.

A few lessons learned in this lifetime:

Not everyone deserves to or knows what to do with power, and that is why teachers/healers/guides must discern between people who use powers for good or evil before they teach all of their wisdom. We can either enhance the earth for the highest good of all, or we can make choices that hurt others in order to only help ourselves or who we serve.

Chapter 2

The Druid Priestess

❖

341 BCE

The current records of the Druids vary by country and were all written by men. Women druids (bandruí) were fierce and mystical, especially in Ireland. Trade to Europe and Britain was in full swing, there were many wealthy families, and it was Ireland's Iron Age, which led to deforestation and the abandonment of nature respect and worship.

For the most part, my clan left me alone. I lived away from the core group, off to myself in the forest next to our village. They only came to get me when there was extreme crop failure or an approaching war, and they could not handle it on their own.

I was too enchanting for the group to gaze upon. I would turn everyone into my slaves, it had once been foretold. I had been named Danu after the beautiful goddess of nature and wisdom. Perhaps that added to my legend as well; or maybe I was Danu, reincarnated from the myths of old.

My beauty was whispered around campfires throughout the land. To be blessed with beauty is a curse and a harsh lesson. If I had been power hungry, I could be the Supreme Leader, with my raven hair flowing down past my knees and my grey blue eyes that held the mist in them. My skin was as white and silky as a pearl, unblemished and smooth. I stood much taller than most others, including most of the men in our village.

I was not excited by the way I looked. I had not craved a family or unlimited power as many women do in our group of seers and healers, magi and oracles. We were the Druids, or so they called us. Some in our group practiced dark offerings in order to gain their gifts and master them. I could not even participate in the weekly sun and moon practices to the gods, nor did I want to. I was not a group person and therein lay most of my trouble.

I had never been a part of them. I was untouchable. Unyielding in my nature and my integrity, they did not know how to make me bow down. Many had tried and many had learned the hard way that I would not be forced to cower before a man or a woman.

I incited fear in their hearts. If I would not birth a daughter to pass my gifts onto, or a son to hand down our ways, if I would not try to become Supreme Leader or some other high position on the council, why was I even a Druid priestess, they hissed to each other.

Not all of them were like that. Some of the other members understood and gave me the respect and peace I desired.

Some of the younger ones joined in the gossip of the elders and would try to get reactions from me, not understanding that I truly was impenetrable.

But all I really craved was my serenity and isolation. I had my plants and a few small animals that kept me company in my small hut. I wanted it that way. There was no judgement from the animals and plants, only love and peace.

Nevertheless, humans could not resist fighting amongst themselves. Owning land, owning each other, owning animals, the list went on and on. Who could have more than the other? Who would be the Master?

Instead of focusing on their hearts and living a life of joy, they had to make war to fill the void, to do as their ancestors had done; continue the death cycle with the incessant need for material goods and power. Always power.

The last time there had been a major war, I was twenty years younger.

I do not think I will live much longer. I have lived over sixty years. Although my energy was still strong, my will to live was leaving this body. The purpose of my life's work had been achieved and I had passed on my knowledge to three students. These students were more like family at this point since I had handpicked and guided them for over fifteen years. They had been orphans as I had been.

This current war had started out like any other – two sides, each thinking that the land belonged to them. Nothing good ever came of wars. Yet we were 'gods' amongst the common folk and if we got involved, it meant one side would be wiped out. However, the fighting was far away from our village and the Supreme Leader had declared we would not be affected, or needed to join the fight to determine a winner.

I was only called in if the high council could not control the outcome, which had happened very rarely in my lifetime. Most of the high leaders were so energetically powerful that they could handle any skirmish.

~~~

Today had started out sunny but by mid-day it had turned into a wet and cold existence.

Two of the High Seer's guards had come to my hut. There were always warriors in our clan, as well as those of us with gifts. They could protect the higher council members from physical threats although that seemed a bit impractical given the various level of powers in each member.

However, if a gifted person could immobilize one of the members energetically, that member would be more susceptible to, let's say, ingesting a poison in their meal or getting run over by a crazed horse.

"Danu, come with us," they demanded.

It was a command from the High Seer, our Supreme Leader, the Holy One, the High Priestess for this century. Her energy was with them.

I nodded my head and followed them closely. Increasingly turning their heads back towards me, they decided I was not walking fast enough.

Each of them grabbed one of my arms and practically lifted me off the ground as they kept their swift pace.

Leaving the forest, I could see we were heading towards the ocean.

They dragged me towards the water to show me what was happening.

From the edge of the cliff, standing on the precipice where I thought it would be so easy to simply jump, I stared down at the rocks below; I envisioned this jumping so that I would not have to take any more orders. I was getting too old for this type of life.

"Look," the smaller guard shouted against the wind as he pointed towards the east.

There were boats, so many boats. So many men. Who were they? This had not been seen by the Great Seer. How was this missed? Were her powers diminishing? It made sense that they would be given her age.

The war was in the south. Not here. Not in their area. It was not allowed.

Some of the ships had made it to the shore. Men with great broadswords were unloading. Metal flashed as the tiny rays of what little sun there was peeking from behind the clouds, landed on their blades, highlighting the truth of how many swords there were invading the clan's shores.

I felt a rush of energy behind me and I knew she was there; the mystic, ancient, wrinkled, High Priestess. The Great Seer. The Supreme Leader. Her given name was Cailleach.

How she kept her energy so high after all of these years was something to ponder on, later, only after this exercise in destroying a massive army was finished.

"Do it, Danu. Now," Cailleach whispered to me.

There was no choice. I had to obey for the survival of my village, as much as I did not like all of the villagers. No matter my personal preference, I did believe that the Druid healing, energy practices and wisdom should continue for many years to come.

I raised my arms above my head and called upon the energy from the heavens. I could feel the energy swirling through my body, creating strong currents of electricity and power. My bare feet in the rocky grass of the cliff started to heat. If someone had touched me at that moment, my skin would feel as hot as fire and the heavy pulsations reverberating throughout my entire body would make them withdraw their hand very quickly.

I heightened my breathing, quickening the energy pulsing from my fingertips to the sky and then circling back again. The air started to swirl around me, and Cailleach's long cape whipped around her legs.

The first crash came. A lightning strike stabbed into the ocean. At first in one area, then the entire ocean was covered with lightning flashes as if being lit up by the sun.

The waves started to rise as thunder shook the entire earth. There would be nowhere to hide from this storm. The men on the beach started running and yelling, but their screams were drowned out by the noise of the storm.

We were too far away to see the faces of the men in boats; nonetheless, I knew their faces showed horror and tears, that there were many whispered prayers and cries for help. Some might be stoic and others might crumble in the face of the gods' anger. Either way, they all knew their time was nigh.

I had created a storm that sent the remaining boats sinking to the bottom of the ocean. Never had a storm been so fierce, it was to be said by the villagers. Never had the earth shook with the fury of the ocean and menacing thunder from the gods.

It could have lasted days or minutes, it mattered not to me. My energy was feeding the storm and the storm driving my energy. I belonged to the heavens, amongst the storms and the clouds, the rains and the calm. The moon and the sun were my loving parents.

My power was stronger than it had ever been before. I could feel it coursing through my veins, willing me to keep going.

Or maybe I secretly wanted this to be my final show? The final display of what I could do before I left this body.

That is when the vision came; unprovoked and spurred on by all of the energy flowing through me.

Cailleach, the Supreme Leader, drinking the blood of a child after harnessing the power from it. The crying of the child right before it died. The smile on Cailleach's face as she drank down the thick, dark liquid while chanting the immortal prayer that was supposedly lost by our ancient teachers long ago. She was the reason so many children had died and gone missing! She was the bringer of death to the villages. And she embraced this dark influence. She had chosen this path long ago, in her attempt to gain more and more power.

I could see her dancing around the stones of the holy circle under a cloudy moon, writhing under the evil energy that took hold of her body, her mind becoming a dark and ugly space as she opened her entire being up to the energy. All of the sudden she stopped dancing and laid naked upon the ground. As she opened her legs up and said, "Take me, my Dark Lord, take all of me. In return, I accept your mission and my eternal life." Her immortality was sealed by giving herself completely to evil.

There came a deep, convoluted laughter and her face changed to a youthful, beautiful woman. A dark shape rose above her and said, "I will give you what you ask for. In return, I plant my seed of death and destruction inside of you. All humans must die so that I can finally rule over this planet in my true form. You will help me fulfill this mission."

She moaned and said, "Yes. I accept you inside of me. I will do your bidding." With her head dropping back and her eyes blinded to truth, she allowed him to enter her womb, her power creation center, the place women in our clan held as the most holy in the body.

He laughed and took her ferociously. The black of his eyes seeped into hers until her once lovely green eyes were now the color of the darkest night. He used her body as a tool to live out his will.

My body recoiled in revulsion at this sight.

My rage at what I had seen fueled the crashing of the waves and the hammering of lightning into the sea. I wanted to look at Cailleach but was certain she would see that I knew.

"Good. You may stop now," the wicked Leader called to me over the noise of my storm.

I could not stop. I must kill her. She would kill the entire earth by using it as a weapon for the Dark King. Her power would ensure he got his wish, not to mention the use of the powers and energy from all of the other Druids combined with hers. They would follow Cailleach because she was the Supreme Leader, because she knew best.

If I took in enough of the storm's energy, I would be able to twist the lightning into a flash of energy that would stop her human heart. It might kill me and possibly the two guards as well.

It was a chance that I was willing to take.

"I'm not finished. They will never come back to this land," I yelled over the deafening crashes of lightning, waves and thunder.

She looked at me then. I could feel her gaze trying to penetrate my mind, but I blocked her wretched effort. I could feel that she wished to head back to our village and didn't understand why I was being so difficult.

I said a quick prayer to my gods and asked for protection as I took on this daughter of evil. There would be no going back once I did this.

But I remembered the cry of the dying child that she had killed in the vision. Cailleach had to go.

Smiling, I grabbed all of the energy vibrating throughout my being and sent it up through the largest lightning bolt that I could observe in the sky. It was close to us on this cliff, ready to crash at any moment into the ground. I steadied it with my mind.

As she shook her head and turned towards her guards, in her slow, seemingly ancient aching walk, Cailleach hollered back at me, "That was the mightiest storm you have ever produced and that I have ever seen. It will be spoken of through the ages."

Seeing only children's blood in her face and body, I immediately seized the massive lightning bolt and sent it through her heart not more than ten steps from where I stood. Her face registered surprise, then disgust, and then she started laughing.

"You stupid girl! You cannot kill me. I am immortal," she howled at me. She pushed her hands out in front of her to battle with me energetically.

But I wasn't finished.

Mustering all of the storm's energy, knowing that trying to hold it all within me could make my body explode, I sent most of it into her heart where the first bolt had struck. Some, I directed to her head and some to her womb. I would destroy it all.

Shock clearly written upon her face, she shrieked at her men, "Grab her!"

They started to run at me but I held out an invisible wall in front of them. I had been practicing this for one year now and I could stop time with an invisible wall built around me if someone meant me harm. The guards were frozen in place.

My energy was draining quickly, almost too quickly. If I hadn't done enough to kill her body, then she would survive due to our healers. If they found her body.

I directed another bolt of lightning from behind her and threw Cailleach off the cliff like a blade of grass in the wind. Her cries echoed up the cliff and she cursed me well into my next lifetime as she fell.

"Your curses have no weight on me and are sent back onto you. I forgive you," I decreed. Forgiving her completely would break her spell from following me into my next lifetime.

Stepping closer to the edge, I peered down onto the jagged rocks below, where her body was lying strewn in pieces and scattered about, as if she were nothing but bits of rag-cloth blown about in a storm.

No, she would not make it back from this one.

I had heard the myth from the priestess that trained me and she had heard it from the one before her and it continued on up the line. If a Druid were to make a deal with the Dark Lord, an agreement of immortality or any other kind of pact, they could only be killed by a natural occurrence such as a storm or drowning, or some other phenomenon, not caused by someone simply trying to murder them or dying of old age.

The fact that I had just proven this myth to be true did not make it any easier. I collapsed onto the ground with no energy left to hold me up.

The guards came running to the side of the cliff and looked down at the dead Supreme Leader. Then they charged straight towards me.

Raising my hand, I asked, "Does it not seem strange to you both that Cailleach lived so long and asked for the babes of the common folk to be brought to her? What did you think she did with them? Do you think that they magically disappeared?"

Eyeing me cautiously, they looked at each other and then the first guard spoke. "We do as we are told. We don't question orders."

I raised an eyebrow and retorted, "If we don't use critical thinking and learn to decipher right from wrong, we become just like the others and then our race dies out as all other ancient wisdom and healing civilizations have before us. Is that what you want?"

The first guard shook his head slowly.

"We can't explain this to the high council, Danu," the second guard somberly replied.

"You won't need to," I countered.

I called forth the crows. Rising out of the forest behind me like a black cloud of a hurricane, one thousand crows descended on her body and feasted until there was nothing left but strips of her long cape and dress.

No man would send me to my death. No high council would interpret today's mishap into a killing.

"Cailleach simply stepped too close to the edge and before you could grab her, as I was busy with the storm and killing an entire invading army, she fell onto the rocks below. You tried to find a way down to her but there was none. You had to wait until I had finished off the enemy. And now you are on your way back to the high council and I am utterly exhausted, waiting here until you come back to mark the place where her body is. By the time you make it back here with the council, I will state that the crows came from nowhere and ate her body until there was nothing left. Which is how it is."

"Convincing story except for one thing - the mind reading by Saira in the council. She will see what really happened," the first guard countered.

"I've already taken care of that," I said assuredly. "Tell me again what happened here today?" I looked at them expectantly, waiting for their replies.

Both guards looked surprised and then repeated my version of the story.

"Are you sure that is what happened," I asked haughtily, as if I were part of the high council.

"Yes. We are sworn to protect the Supreme Leader at all costs. We were not fast enough to save her misstep but we also thought she was invincible and immortal," they both responded in unison.

"Invincible and immortal? What would give you such an idea? After all, Cailleach was only a powerful Druid."

"We had seen things that led us to question her immortality," said the second guard.

"I am sure that what you saw in her service was quite fascinating. Before we finish this discussion, please run back to the village and alert the high council. I will wait here while you bring others to help recover her body, or at least mark the spot where her body fell. Go!" I commanded as I waved them away.

They both turned and started towards the village. Who knows how long it would take them to get back here with all of the others?

Putting a mental block on their warrior minds that could not be penetrated by Saira was a skill only possessed by me for a time. I had helped others develop this skill to obstruct the intrusions of the Supreme Leader and Saira; they could enter into the mind without permission and see a person's true motivations. The belief that they were allowed to do this for the betterment of our clan made me find a way to thwart them.

Being an outcast had led others to my door for dealings outside of our village.

When someone wanted a commoner as a lover, or to hide an outing to a dance in a neighboring town, or a drunken escapade that led to a fatherless child, or to find the woman of their dreams by traveling far away from the clan, they all came to me. And I never turned one of them away unless they meant evil. Very few of them did.

Most of them simply wanted a certain level of freedom, not dictated by a high council or Supreme Leader.

Liberation was desired and achieved by some of them. Even among all of this power, energy, healing and being labeled as gods, there was a primal need for some normalcy, for the experience of this lifetime to be in human terms.

To love and feel as a human does. Both are the greatest gifts.

Not living buried in a village, obeying orders, healing and helping, but never really living.

This is why some of our younger people had started going out for walks and never coming back. Who could blame them?

All of this pondering I was doing lying on my back by the cliff's edge was making me ache. Waiting for the guards and the high council was a nightmare. My energy was depleted.

There would be no more wars for me. No more training students. Definitely no more mental blocks or romantic conquests for me to help the villagers.

I could feel that my end was coming. Unsure of the exact moment or what it would look like, I decided to sit up. It most likely was not from the passage of time on the rocky edge of a cliff.

A sound reverberated and I looked towards the forest.

Marching out of the woods, with the two guards leading the small group, came the high council. Not able to see their faces, I could feel the energy of the group: some were stunned and muted, others suspicious, and two were secretly rejoicing as they felt *they* now had the chance to become Supreme Leader.

As they got closer, I could see that the ten of them looked as old as I felt. Only one was younger than I, aged fifty-five.

Shakily, I rose to my feet but my energy was completely diminished - next to nothing left at all. This had better be quick because I needed to rest.

The wind chose that moment to burst upon the scene, making my dark hair gust around my body in rising and falling waves. Surely I looked like a mythical enchantress, which would only incense one of the members of the council named Saira, the unscrupulous mind reader. She wanted my youthful countenance and beauty and no matter what spells she tried, she never altered herself for the better.

As they reached me, they asked where the body was.

The guards pointed down directly behind me. I turned my body to that point but could not seem to even muster the energy to point my finger to the location.

"All I see is a scrap of cloth, Danu," stated one of the council. He turned to look at me with an eyebrow raised.

"Well that would make sense. A flock of crows came and flew directly below. Due to my lack of energy from demolishing a warmongering army, I could barely keep from collapsing into a deep sleep, let alone keep watch over her body so crows wouldn't get at it," I answered warily.

"Always with an excuse, Danu! Never thinking of others! Cailleach's poor body! Now, how will we have the funeral pyre and give the gods *her* burning body," screeched Saira while she shook her forefinger at me.

I gently eased myself back onto the ground and into a sitting position. This might be a long talk.

Looking at Saira, I addressed her softly, "I'm sure we could arrange a horse or cow instead for the funeral pyre. They are a large enough sacrifice for the gods. I can't think right now. I truly need to rest."

Saira stared at me in disgust. "You always have been so lazy."

"Come now, Saira. Without her, we would all be overrun by those thousands of men. That was the largest army we had ever seen in our lifetimes. She is vital to our clan. Stop squawking at her. The council must decide who will be next and what actions to take for this unexpected happenstance. We must convene to the altar," asserted Emrys, an honest and warmhearted 90 year-old high council member.

He spun on his heels and headed towards the village.

Everyone started to follow him but Saira. She gazed down at me with hatred bursting from her eyes like two dark orbs of the deepest ocean.

"There will be a reckoning. I have seen your demise, Danu," she whispered.

"I have felt it too. I used too much energy today," I agreed.

She inhaled sharply. "No, there is more to come. This day will go down in history."

"Saira, I don't know why you loathe me so much. If it's simply a balm for your dark soul, you should know that I really do not care what you say or the fear you are trying to instill in my mind. I am quite content to leave the earth at this time."

"You always had to be above me! Always the most beautiful, always the detached and unshakeable marble queen," she heatedly continued. "Why couldn't you just die when you were supposed to?"

"If I cared about your plots and schemes, I would be living in another land. But fortunately for all of us, you can barely cast a spell and maintain it. Energetically, you are a barren, decaying old bag of bones. Go bother someone else," I countered as I slowly made my way to my feet.

"Every man has been enchanted by you. In our youth and even now, they only see you. I could have been happy once, I could have been loved. But you ruined it all. You stole my beloved!"

Regarding her rising ire with disdain, I decided it was time to head back to my hut.

She certainly seemed to be losing her grip on reality. I had never been with any man, let alone someone she would have loved. That thought made me want to vomit but there was nothing in my belly. I needed food. I needed some energy.

Sending a prayer up to the gods for patience, I gave her a piercing look and tersely ground out, "I have no idea what you are yelling about. I am going home." With that said, I turned and started my journey towards my little hut in the woods.

"I will show you! You will never be rid of me," she screamed at my back.

The gods only know what she would plan now. Her little intrigues throughout the village, and even within the arena of politics, had been funny to most of the citizens. Most were cottoned onto quite quickly but I was certain there were a few that had ended with people dying.

She was not a forgiving woman. Nor was she out for the good of the village.

She was only out for herself, as she had been since we were young. And apparently, I had stolen her beloved.

As I wracked my brain for any memories of a man even approaching me, for mine was not the energy mere men could even come near, I could not remember any man from our village hazarding this. There had been only two in my lifetime who had even risked my anger by asking for my hand.

They had both been warrior kings from bordering lands. Both had heard of my beauty and powers, and decided they should try to marry me, not for me, myself and I, mind you. But for my power that would surely increase their lands and wealth.

Not understanding that I knew it was not to be my path in this lifetime, they thought marriage to a king was every woman's aspiration. They considered me a mighty, albeit humble, beautiful Druid princess. There was no marrying me or even getting close to my heart, although both of them tried for a long period of time before they gave up.

Both of them were quite handsome and charming, radiating masculine energy and authority. One was dark; dark skin tanned by the sun, dark hair like midnight, tall and muscular with amazing grey eyes like a stormy sky. The other was light; light, blonde hair, golden skin, tall and muscular as well with the bluest eyes that I had ever seen.

When they had come into my village at the same time, to pursue me on the same day, I knew the gods were laughing at me. They were telling me my choice: the dark side or the light side. I was young and of child bearing age, beautiful without rival, and coming into the full expression of my gifts and powers.

I could discern that the true choice was not between the men. I had known that marriage was not my path since I was small; I had never dreamed of a husband and children. My visions were consumed with gaining full access to my genius and passing on what I could to other talented beings that contained a certain energetic bloodline that could not be tempted over to the dark side.

There was always a choice in which way a Druid chose to practice their powers. Some of the Druids chose the dark side and some chose the light side. It was your choice to make; which side you connected to and felt the most power from.

Since I had always wanted unlimited possibilities regarding my energetic powers, I listened to the stories of the elder Druids. I weighed out the options, including the usually deadly repercussions when someone chose the dark side; (their strange deaths were witnessed by these elders).

A person could have what they wanted quickly with the dark side but it usually killed them after a short time. If it didn't kill them, their powers became uncontrollable and similar to a mortal royal, they became obsessed with greed, immortality and more power.

Despite the beauty of these two men, and the safety it might offer me, I decided against both of them. They considered it a challenge and kept lavishing me with gifts, baskets of herbs from far off places, and all manners of adoration. I continued to reject everything except the herbs; I could not turn away from the chance to learn more or heal with unknown remedies.

Subsequently, they both called me the "Marble Queen"; heartless and cold, whom no man could love and be devoted to. They left me alone after months of their one-sided courting, leaving many in the Druid village confused as to how I could refuse either of them. It would have furthered the connections and added value for the community. How could I be so short sighted and selfish?

Even a meeting with the Supreme Leader hadn't changed my mind. She didn't understand that I could not be persuaded into using dark or light magic, or into any marriage irrespective of the man and his power; I would make my own decisions.

Perhaps it was one of these kings that the harpy Saira was screeching about. Did she fancy herself loved by one of them while they were in the village? Had she given herself to one of them?

In her delusional mind, notwithstanding their very public wooing of me, if she had given herself to one of them, she would have seen that person as hers. Forever.

Regardless of the fact I had refused both of them and taken neither one into my home or bed, she would have blamed me as the perpetrator when they left.

Sighing with exhaustion and exasperation, I shook my head. Some people were so far gone it was a true wonder that they made it out of adolescence. I wouldn't call it a miracle, because surely there were better life circumstances than to be living in a fantasy land where a man loves a woman just because she slept with him.

~~~

I stumbled into my herb filled sanctuary that I called home.

The fire was going, thank the gods for my lovely apprentice Kristine, with a pot of stew hanging over its side, warmed but not burnt. She was the sweetest apprentice I could have ever asked for. She had made sure my home was welcoming after my harrowing day.

Hungrily, I grabbed a bowl and broke off some bread. I would need my strength. I could feel the hatred coming at me.

Soon, said the voice inside of me. I sighed and finished my meal.

Now it was time to rest for a few hours while the unrest in the village was stirred up by the vicious and vindictive Saira. There was no time for me to try and heal any of the village energy. I was too tired and weak and would save my life-force for what was coming.

~~~

Awakened by loud voices outside of my little hut, I rose from my bed. There came a pounding on my door.

"Open up, Danu. We are taking you before the high council," a booming voice pierced through the wooden door.

"On what grounds," I inquired.

"We are only here to escort you. The summons from the council must be obeyed," the male voice resonated throughout my home.

Let's get this over with, my heart said. No point in arguing with this lackey. He was not the one in charge. It would be interesting to see who had claimed command over the council. Had they really let insane Saira win? All of them knew she was unbalanced after all of these years; that's why they had kept her on the council, to keep an eye on her.

Pushing the door open, I stepped out into the yard. There were six men waiting, two with torches and four holding swords. As if a sword could stop me.

I laughed quietly to myself because, truthfully, a sword most likely could stop me right now since my energy was so low. And because I knew my time was coming. I welcomed my death.

"I will follow you," I stated softly.

"Good. Let's go."

He led the way through the village and to the meeting area of the council; the stone walls and dark interior of the court where people were judged for their crimes or actions, and where all decisions were made for the good of our small Druid clan.

It was not a soothing structure for any person being led there.

The large fire burning in the middle of the room lit up the faces of the council; each face with its own problems etched all over it, with a few showing the desire to be elsewhere at this particular moment. I felt compassion for those faces.

Saira had the only smiling face of the group. She had won some power play, there was no doubt of that, and I was about to find out just how big of a victory for her it had been.

No other people from the village were there. Two of the guards had come inside with me but the other four stood outside the door.

I pondered if they were keeping me in or the villagers out?

Saira triumphantly began, "Danu, you have been accused of killing the High Priestess. We are unsure of your motives or the whereabouts of her body." She paused. "Did you purposely kill the High Priestess, our Supreme Leader known as Cailleach?"

"You can't find a body because the crows ate it. What elaborate scheme have you hatched up now, Saira? What accusations do you bring for me murdering the Supreme Leader," I asked, staring at her with compassion. I felt sorry for her, harboring such hate for her entire life.

The other members shifted uncomfortably in their seats. I had struck a nerve.

Saira laughed. "We all know that you are guilty. The guards don't remember anything; they don't remember her falling, and don't remember even coming into the village to tell all of us about Cailleach's death. You infiltrated their minds, and now you want us to believe that you had nothing to do with her death?"

Looking at Saira and then glancing at the other council members, I chose to remain humble.

I replied as I stared back at Saira, "For someone that declared she would never die, I'm surprised you think that I, the extremely isolated, herbal healer, the person that is called on again and again to help you win wars that cannot be won without my energetic meddling, would be able to do that. Let me guess. After sinking more ships than I've ever seen in my life, killing more warriors than I could count, and winning a war that would have destroyed this entire island, I somehow had the energy to overpower the High Priestess; the woman with over one hundred years of energy and power, the woman that by some means never died despite her increasing age?"

"Yes! This is what you did! You overpowered her. You killed her," Saira shouted as she glanced around at the other council members, nodding at them to try and convince them to agree with her. A few did. But most of them stared at her as if she had lost her mind.

"I'm not finished," I exclaimed. "After using more energy than I had in my being, more energy than I have ever used in my entire life of battles won for this village or by saving the crops on this entire island when everyone would have starved to death, and having found the energy to murder Cailleach who, mind you, could always tell when she was in danger or someone was trying to kill her, I then was able to summon the energy to call the birds to eat up her flesh, which is not one of my current skill sets, and immediately have even more energy to erase the memories of her guards? This is what you are claiming? Is everyone on this council in agreement that this is what I did?"

As I glanced around at their solemn faces, I could tell that they had all, except for Saira, been swayed by the impossibility of the picture I had painted.

Saira was nodding her head vigorously, as if this would be the saving grace to her accusations.

I continued, "So not only am I the weapon this village needs to survive wars and onslaughts, famine and destruction, I now have unlimited energetic capabilities wherein I can take down the Supreme Leader at my whim and anything else I desire at the same time? Wow, I truly am a marvelous being! If this is what you think I am capable of, you should put me to death immediately," I said with a wry smile.

Everyone on the council now showed some fear. They knew they had overstepped by allowing Saira this biased accusatory meeting.

Now they understood just how unsafe it was for any of them to have powers which exceeded Saira's powers. They could all be sitting in my place right now with some story concocted of why they should be put to death.

What might have made sense to them in the beginning now made no sense at all. There was no way that one Druid had the power to do all that I had done in the course of a few hours. It was not energetically possible and had never been done before. Nobody had that much energy or skill.

The silence in the room was telling.

Emrys finally spoke. "I think I speak for the majority of us when I say that we do not believe you are capable of this heinous act. In fact, we are not sure that she did not fall as you said she did. We do know that no-one besides the High Priestess is allowed near you when you are destroying hordes of men bent on taking over this fair land; for being near you at that time can have consequences as we were told by the High Priestess. The fact that Cailleach had guards present could explain why they have no memory of anything that happened, before or after the Supreme Leader's fall. There are too many variables unaccounted for."

"You've got to be joking! Danu is guilty! She did it! Why do you not believe me?" screamed Saira, her voice hitching up into a high pitched, ear-piercing shrill. "You all are hoodwinked by her beauty. She is a serpent, she is of the ancient dark magic and she deserves to die!"

Another council member spoke, "Saira, you are not the Supreme Leader nor have you been appointed to preside over this court. We are all sitting as equals on this council. We will have a show of hands. Who here believes that the Supreme Leader was murdered by Danu, who willingly stands before us?"

Only one raised their hand, Saira. Her face contorted with rage. When she looked at me, her eyes spoke volumes. She was consumed with madness; a burning need to see my death.

"As we are all in agreement, barring one, this council releases you and hereby declares that you are innocent of the charge that has been brought against you of murdering our High Priestess and Supreme Leader. Please return to your home. The guards will escort you for your safety," one of the oldest council members proclaimed, with a meaningful look at Saira.

"I appreciate your ruling and your fair and level-headed approach, council members. Thank you for your service to our village," I replied as a reminder to what I had just done for the village on the edge of the cliff. "I wish you vision and good faith in choosing the next Supreme Leader/High Priest or Priestess for our community."

I bowed to them and turned to take my leave, knowing the guards would escort me on my way home.

Who knew how much of the village Saira had spewed her accusations to? They would escort me to ensure the villagers did not try to harm me.

I noticed that one of the guards listened as the oldest member spoke softly to him. Then the guard nodded before following me out the door.

~~~

That turned out in a way I had not anticipated, yet I had neither the energy nor the will to contemplate it. The weariness of my entire soul was weighing heavily on my body. The hours, or perhaps days, it would have taken to explain about the Supreme Leader being giving her power to the Dark Lord and blood sacrifice of babies…I did not have those hours.

I stumbled slightly and one of the guards that had been inside the council chamber caught me before I fell. He kept his arm around my waist for the remainder of the journey back to my hut in the woods.

Grateful for this assistance, I warmly said goodbye to the guard once we reached my home.

"Kai is staying to guard your door tonight," the guard motioned to another guard so that he stepped forward. "The council thinks Saira might try something."

"I am grateful for the watch," I nodded at Kai. To the other guard I said, "I appreciate your help." I smiled at him as I closed my door and turned to the tranquility and silence of my hut.

The fire was faintly burning so I threw a log onto it to get it flaming higher again. I would need the heat that it would provide on this night.

Although Saira's accusations were true, I would not admit to the council all of my gifts. If they knew everything I had done, including the invisible wall, they would use it for their gain. I did not trust them to not be swayed by Saira or any other evil-minded person.

There was no need to share that knowledge with them. That would die with me.

How was I to die then? I had thought undoubtedly they would find me guilty and burn or drown me.

If today was not the day, then why had I felt it?

Was my energy so misplaced? Was my inner guidance too far gone? Was this what happened with age mixed with one afternoon of extreme energy use, after being powerful and gifted for too long?

I frowned. I knew not what the answer was, and could think about this tomorrow. Tonight, I needed sleep.

But first, I arranged my table area and set a quick trap. My energy never lied.

Falling onto my bed exhausted, I said a prayer of protection without belief. What did I want to be protected against?

~~~

The door shutting gently woke me up.

Somebody was in here with me. I listened intently for any sound, but nothing came. Maybe the guard had gotten warm by the fire and then left.

I strained my hearing for a few more minutes until my eyelids fluttered as I drifted back to sleep.

~~~

A searing pain ripped through my stomach, as if a knife had been driven through my skin and was digging circles around and around into my abdomen, seeking to pull out my insides.

My eyes flew open and lit upon Saira's frenzied face. I moaned as my hands flew to my stomach, catching upon the knife she had twisted into my belly.

Lifting her hands away and covering her mouth with one hand, she started giggling. "I have won, you see. You thought you could beat me but you never will. You will die now, Danu."

Her laughter continued to grow louder and louder as what little remained of my energy leaked from the gaping wound in my stomach.

Looking up at her, I could see that she thought she had won.

"Saira, is this the knife from my table?" I questioned her, trying to breathe slowly through the pain.

"Yes, you fool. I killed the guard with his own sword after I knocked him unconscious while he was in a foggy stupor that I placed over his mind. And then I waited while you went back to sleep, because I knew that you had heard the door open and close. I wanted you to think that you were alone and safe. Your knife was just sitting on the table, beckoning to me. Now you will die. Although it will be slow since I only put it in your belly, and I wanted you to suffer as I have; a pain deep in your belly that you cannot be rid of. But that will all end with your death."

One thing about Saira, she loved to brag about her cleverness.

I smiled up at her menacingly ugly face. "Ah, Saira. And why do you think the knife beckoned to you? Why would I ever leave my knife out on the table? Look at your hands," I instructed.

For a few seconds, disbelief registered on her face. When she looked down at her black hands, she started wailing. The blackness was working its way up her arms and spreading from her mouth along the bottom part of her face and into her neck.

"No, no, no! You murdering witch! No!" she howled. "This is not how it was supposed to happen! I saw it in my vision. You would die and I would become Supreme Leader. Why?"

"You know that I could not let you become leader after I worked so hard to get rid of the darkness we had before. Cailleach danced with black magic and so do you. Don't worry. The poison should kill you quickly," I gave her a weak smile as I felt the blood pouring sluggishly out of my body.

Saira tried to escape towards the door but fell on her face. The poison had worked its way to her heart by now. Her breathing would stop soon. The sound of her gasping for air told me that her death would be within a few moments.

There would be no time for me to give Kristine the invisible wall technique. No time to show her what would happen to this small Druid village if the dark magic was not contained. Had I done enough for this place? I had killed so many in service to my clan, to my village. Was it enough and would they survive into the next century?

However, that was no longer my worry. I was at peace. I was free.

I was going home.

I closed my eyes and breathed in the last breath in this body, thankful of the bright light and warmth that surrounded me for my homeward journey.

A few lessons learned in this lifetime:

Energetically and spiritually advanced people have a choice between good (positive) or evil (negative). We all have supernatural powers and the power within to create our reality. Each person in each lifetime must choose to either use their gifts to help people or use them to hurt people. When a person is so powerful and destructive, you can either stand by and watch them destroy innocents or you can use your gifts to destroy them. But karmic retribution is real and must be paid in this lifetime or the next.

Chapter 3

The Mongolian Warlord

❖

1221 CE

Genghis Khan ruled Mongolia with an iron fist during this time. He was the first ruler/emperor and united the nomadic Mongol tribes and warlords. His numerous ruthless campaigns extended from Poland to China and led to millions of civilian deaths and destruction of towns, landscapes and entire tribes. His warlords were notoriously as savage and ruthless as he was, and they would find themselves swiftly killed if there were any doubts as to their loyalty.

There was nothing like the open range and the smell of fear in the air. The raids were going well but too long had I been away from home. I missed my wife. I did not miss my children. They were irritating most of the time. I cannot wait for them to be old enough to be married off.

I have spent many years wandering these lands. There is a freedom in the land and the knowing of it. Such open space, and when I close my eyes, I feel as if I am the eagle. I am flying and looking down on other humans, blinking slowly and spreading my wings to soar even higher.

The times have been changing. I can feel it.

I am the mighty Batuhan, the captain of this marauding party. My Kahn sent me out to gather slaves and food from a tribe that settled too close to our land.

I do not argue with what I'm told and I'm amazing at what I do. I am a much feared and respected warlord and warrior. Men obey me and the Kahn trusts me.

My name will be passed down for generations and my sons will be proud.

If my wife would have sons. She has only had daughters. Daughters are very pretty but she must have a son soon or I must find a new wife.

It does not matter. Either way, I am coming back rich from the raids and there are always ways to dispose of wives. If needed. But that should not be the case here.

When I was smaller, my father showed me the ways of raiding. It was easier to get information if you spoke other languages, so from him I learned a few as well. There was no shame in learning all you could about people that traded in your lands or wanted to learn about your people.

But I have always belonged to the land. To sleep outdoors and be at peace.

I am never allowed privacy when I sleep in my own tent. I love to have sex with my wife but not with three daughters clinging onto her dress and hanging around our sleeping area. When I had left her this time, she was most likely pregnant. There was no way she could not be.

~~~

The open air of this place took these thoughts away. I glanced around.

Land spread out in all directions. I could not wait to roast fresh meat over a fire in the middle of a mountain range. There is nothing better than an animal freshly caught, roasting, and the knowing that you are free. At least for that night.

Staring at the intruder camp in the distance, I wondered if they could sense we were coming. We will catch these people and make them slaves. Their men are out hunting and possibly raiding further west.

We don't raid too much west anymore. East is more open and free. There are too many different peoples to the west. Too many places to get caught unawares.

"Alright, men. Let's start the fires and then gather all the women. We only take the children if they are strong and close to age. The rest stay here for their fathers to see their shame," I said to the four warriors closest to me. They were my most feared warriors and the next four in command if something happened to me.

"My lord, are you sure we shouldn't just kill the children? It would make the others fall in line easier," one of my feared commanders asked me. He always wanted to kill everyone. He was more bloodthirsty than I, in my youth.

"You do as you please. I will not answer for your actions. We are to bring many usable or sellable slaves and great provisions back to the Kahn. You know the rules," I said.

"Yes, my lord. Thank you. We will make you proud," he answered and walked away to go ready the other raiders.

Make me proud, we shall see about that. I give my men a bit of freedom or else they would resent me. I do not care what they do as long as we come back with the goods and many slaves to make our people proud and strong.

For my men, life is just beginning. They are young and carefree.

I had killed so many people that I had lost count. It was the way of life, the show of strength mattered more than peace. There was no time to wonder if I had done something wrong or what that even meant.

I was living my purpose, what I had been shown as a boy by my father, and I was fulfilling my destiny. When it was my time to go, it was my time.

Killing a human meant nothing to me. Protecting my people meant everything.

The world was getting smaller. New people everywhere, new foods, new languages, new religions.

My children would see expansion on another level. I was slightly envious of all the innovative weapons that would come in the next hundred years. I felt them coming but didn't know from where.

I listened to my old mother. It was amazing she was still alive. She had much wisdom and saw visions that I could not. She had spoken to me of the new war machines; images that I could not begin to fathom. There was something eerie yet comforting about them. I would be dead when they came around but maybe one of my children will create them. It was possible.

But it was time now. Time for the raid.

I always rode with my men. No leader worth anything stayed behind.

~~~

My horse loved to race into battle. I could feel him beneath me, the warrior in him becoming one with the warrior in me. He was the best horse I had ever had.

As we thundered towards the encampment, every person turned towards us.

Screams and running commenced. Nobody would be safe on this day.

We slaughtered what men we saw, and my men gathered up the women, tying them together. A few of the older children were taken as well. There were not many of them.

Nodding at my next in command, he grabbed the rope that linked the women together and got on his horse.

He led the slaves away with a group of my men, back towards our camp. I steered my horse to the front of the small party. I was on the lookout for any approach as well as being their leader.

The other men would do their worst on the remaining children. It was not for me to say.

The women were crying and moaning. It was getting louder the more steps they took away from their camp. They were possibly sending up prayers to their ancestors. They knew that their children back in the camp were being slaughtered.

I had no sympathy. Their men should not have left them. It was such a tiny group of people, and their men should have known they were in someone's territory. This lack of knowledge was a grave error in judgment.

As we continued on the journey at a brisk pace, the sky began to darken. There would be rain. A storm would be fitting for today.

I spurred my horse for a quicker march back to our tents, putting some distance in between myself and the howling slaves.

~~~

The women were trying to sorrowfully wail and scream the entire way back. My ears and head were starting to ache even though I was further ahead.

Rolling my eyes, I steered my horse back towards my men.

I have had enough of this. I usually could block it all out but with the storm approaching, the energy seemed stifling.

The extreme sadness from the women was having an effect on me.

Glancing at my men, I could see a few of them were staring straight ahead in a daze. One of them almost walked his horse into a ravine before I grabbed his reins and jerked his horse's head upright to stop.

The horses even looked overcome.

It was time to interrupt.

"Wake up, men! We need to stay focused. Let's keep the pace and look forward to our feast tonight," I declared loudly.

I saw on their faces that they registered what I had said with their eyes but did not move a muscle.

What was going on? Were these women witches? Why was this happening?

"STOP!" I screamed. I scrambled from my horse and started ripping strands of cloth from an extra tunic. "Come here, men!"

They slowly gathered around me similar to drunken men stumbling towards a campfire.

Astonished, I dropped the cloth to the ground before I punched each one of them in the face, making them stumble backwards or flat on their backside.

My fist was oozing blood when I was done with the twelve of them.

"Tighten these around their mouths. No more of this witchcraft!" I said vehemently, handing out the strips of cloth. This should stop the insanity.

The men did as they were bid but seemed to struggle with the simple task.

Women were thrashing about, trying to keep their mouths from being bound.

Ah! They were witches. Just as I thought! They were casting spells with their wailing. What power to behold! I will tell the Kahn they needed to be put to death upon arrival. This was unacceptable in the Kahn's kingdom.

It started to rain as the last woman was silenced with the muzzle. This would be a beautiful ride back to camp. Only another hour.

Oh, glorious silence!

~~~

Approaching the camp, it became clear that the spell had worn off. Perhaps the rain had woken the men up as well.

My mind was strong enough to overcome their witchcraft. However, what would have happened if all the men were gathered. If I had not been aware…as the men back at the enemy camp were currently.

Why had none of them caught up to us yet?

Thirteen of us are holding fifty witch women captive. Thirty of my men were behind us. It would be useful if we could all return to the Kahn together.

Were the children as powerful? This was not something I had considered.

In fact, I had only heard stories about tribes with this type of sorcery. My father's father had come into contact with one. It did not end well for his men. Most of them had killed themselves in the middle of the night.

There was nothing I could do now but wait.

Trying to compete with the thunderstorm, I bellowed at my men, "Put them all around that tree." I pointed to the central large tree, "Facing outwards. They will not be protected by the covering of a tent. If they die from the storm, they die. Four men to guard them at all times. Four hour shifts. Keep your eyes on them, they have evil ways."

The men snapped to attention and did as I had bid them.

I would stay awake. There was only one way to know what would happen. Apparently, I was the only one with a mind strong enough to withstand witchcraft. At least my grandfather had four others with him who did not fall to the spells of witches and the five of them had all made it back to their home after their witch encounter.

~~~

Each hour, I checked on all of my men. They seemed to be manning their post or sleeping.

Still, the others had not returned and they should have by now. This was not good news.

Had I lost 30 men to sorcery? This was worse than losing them in battle. I would be proud to lose them in battle; I had trained them all myself. And I could spare no man to go back and check.

Staring at the captives from my tent opening, I knew that there had to be a leader; one that was stronger than the others. If I could single her out and kill her, all would be well. They would understand that their witchery would not prevail.

Which one is it? They all looked the same. None of them were looking up. Heads were down due to the rain.

I could wait. Someone will point her out with some small action, a small head movement or a few seconds of eye contact.

Walking out of my tent in a hurry when I saw one of my men nodding off instead of watching the women, I slapped him awake and said, "Remove yourself and put the next man on guard."

Hiking my voice up even more, I bellowed to the other guards, "There is no sleeping on duty tonight. The other men behind us will not be returning. Something happened to them because they should have been here already."

The man looked alarmed as he rushed off to grab his replacement. The three other men seemed to look at each other with wariness creeping into their eyes. Then they looked at the slaves with hatred.

None of the women were looking up at this exchange but that did not mean they did not hear what I had said.

Who knew if these women could speak our language? If so, we were in more trouble than I wanted to admit.

I had to test it.

I marched next to the circle of women and stood in front of a pretty one that could have been the leader. She was middle aged, not young but not old, and looked very relaxed for her current situation.

"Stand up! Stand up right now," I barked at her.

She looked up at me and blinked, water running down her face from the rain.

I resumed my heightened tone, "I know you can understand me. Up! NOW!"

As she continued to look at me blankly, I decided a show of force would demand the leader show herself.

I grabbed a fistful of hair to the girl on her right, forcing the girl to stand. This jerked the tied hands of the could-be leader and the old woman on the other side of the girl, as they were all tied to the same rope.

The potential head witch's eyes widened as she saw me remove my knife from its sheath.

I held the knife against the girl's throat, "I will kill her unless you stand up."

She stood up straightaway staring at the girl's belly, yanking up the hands of the woman on her left. Good for me, I thought, as I glanced down. The girl I held was pregnant. I released her and let her fall to the ground.

"Untie this woman," I said to the closest guard, pointing at the head witch. "She is coming to my tent to speak with me."

The man started untying her from the others and then tied her hands separately. He led her behind me into my tent. I gestured for her to be placed on the carpet in front of my sleeping cushion.

After he had gone, I stared at her. She was very pretty although quite disheveled from the long march and the rain.

Tactics with women, I reminded myself. Never easy but it must be done.

"Tell me your name." I spoke as kindly as I could, considering she was a witch.

"My name is not important," she retorted, throwing her head back and staring me in the eyes.

Ah, here was the power. I had guessed correctly! Thank you, ancestors!

"I am Batuhan. Are you the leader of this group, witch?"

"I am no witch. I am a healer. And I am not a leader," she stated with a certainty fixed on her face.

"As my other men have not come back, and witnessing the stupor you placed my men into on the way here, I will say your entire clan is a cluster of witches," I countered.

"You can say what pleases you," she rejoined.

This could be a long night, I thought to myself.

"Now that you are captured, what do you think will happen," I asked her.

"It does not matter. I will survive. So will my people."

"If I could make it easier on you, would you tell me your name and why your people are in our territory," I calmly inquired.

"It does not matter if you make it easier on me, Batuhan. There is nothing to tell. Our people were starving in our last home. We moved because we are nomads, as all tribes are. We had heard stories of the lushness and bounty of this land. Facing a new warlord would be less troublesome than half of our people dying off from hunger, as we had been doing for the past two years," she answered.

Her eyes had remained filled with longing. Of what, I wondered. Of her old home?

I remained silent. What could I say to her? That they had picked the wrong territory?

I knew nothing of starvation as my tribe was vastly prosperous and had been for over one hundred years. I could not say what it would drive me to do if my people were starving.

"You could make me your concubine. I will not mind," she boldly stated. Her gaze penetrated my soul. She knew I found her attractive.

My wife would kill her.

I laughed. "My wife would not consent to that."

"Your wife cannot bear you sons. I can," she replied with her head held in a proud way that stated she knew she would have only sons.

Blood pumped to my loins. Well, this was an intriguing twist I was not prepared for.

How would she know that I wanted a son more than anything else in the world? Eight years with my wife and only three daughters to show for it. I was getting no younger.

I could take her now. Agree to this. Nobody would know. I could keep her as a servant and if she didn't have my son, I could trade her off.

My wife would understand eventually since she could not have a son. There would be some fighting, but she would see my way. I was the warlord and master after all. My wife was lucky she was still here after eight years of no sons. I loved my wife, but this could solve my problems. Or indeed add to them.

Nonetheless, I did not trust this woman. She definitely was a witch.

She smiled, "I am not a witch. I heal people from their sicknesses which begin in the spirit. I can see your sickness. You are a brutal murderer and warmonger and it haunts your soul, Batuhan. That is why your wife has borne you no sons. She refuses to pass your lineage on. The murdering bloodline will stop with you."

I slammed my fist down on the table. "You will be silent. I will not listen to your nonsense. What has been done to my other men?"

"Your other men will be here soon. Why are you worried about them?" she probed.

"They are late. It should not have taken them long to finish their business and be directly behind. Even with the rain."

She stared at me with one eyebrow raised.

I heard a yell out in the camp. I could not leave her to search my tent and find a weapon to murder me with. As I grabbed her to rush out of the tent, she rubbed her body against me and whispered, "You will come for me this night and I will show you what it is to fly the way you have dreamed. My name is Aigiarn and you will remember me for the rest of your life."

Shaking my head and pulling her outside, I searched the night for my men.

"Lord, the other men are approaching. They sent a man ahead," the guard declared while staring at Aigiarn. He looked frightened by her.

"Send me that man. And tie her back up with the other prisoners. Don't forget to bind her mouth." I handed her over and marched back to my tent.

As I waited patiently for the man to appear, I checked around to discern if she had stolen anything. My few items on the top of my miniature folding table were still there, and besides my bed and sitting area, there was nothing Aigiarn could have taken small enough to murder me with.

The man sent ahead of the rest of my men burst through my curtains and stopped abruptly before me. He was sweating and very out of breath.

"What is wrong with you," I said as I cautiously examined him at a distance, wary of getting too close to him.

"My lord, I am not sure," he replied. "All of the men are feeling ill. Some say there was a virus in the enemy camp. Others are saying it was sorcery."

His eyes kept dancing to and fro, looking off into space one minute and then landing on floating objects that only he could see, as if his mind could not control where his gaze cavorted.

"What exactly happened at that camp? Why are you so late in getting here?" I demanded.

I was losing patience with the entire situation.

Had there been no gold or silver, no expensive trading items, no oils or spices, nothing of value in their camp besides fifty women and girls that were seemingly more trouble than they were worth?

The Kahn would not be happy with this pitiful haul, which meant that I would be answering to an angry Genghis Kahn and dealing with the aftermath.

"As we started to kill the children and search for hidden goods, a mist arose from nowhere and we could see nothing. We started to form a circle to better protect ourselves, and darkness came upon us instantly. Then we heard it or rather, heard nothing. The world went completely silent. Within one minute, we were attacked by their men. They all must use some type of witchcraft.

We could barely see their swords until they were right in front of us. We were deaf to their movements. They attacked us for three hours. We held our ground and occasionally killed one of them. Five of our men died. The only thing that saved us was the prayers we said to our ancestors. These prayers must have weakened their powers because when the rain came, we were able to see them all and finish them off. There were twenty in all and we chopped their heads off and removed their hearts to end the sorcery. We would have burned them but everything was wet," he added.

His entire body was shaking, as if he had a fever he could not feel but his limbs convulsed without his awareness.

"You need rest. Remove yourself and find food and sleep," I commanded. He was another one to keep an eye on.

'What else could go wrong tonight? How could I bring back these witches to my home, to my Kahn?' I thought. They would infect everyone until we were all dead and wiped from the earth.

Why would Aigiarn offer herself to me? Does she worry about death? No, she was a witch. Dying was the least of her concerns.

She wanted to exact revenge. If she thought she could hypnotize me into doing her bidding, she would go undetected until she could murder us all. Or make us murder each other? I have no idea how powerful she could be, although it seemed as long as she was silenced, she could not make the spells.

This meant she was not as powerful as she wished and, that if I removed all of their tongues, they would be useful as servants or easily traded. Then the expedition was not a complete waste after all.

After another hour, the remaining twenty-four men arrived. They looked as if demons had possessed them.

"Captain, come with me," I ordered the warrior who had been left in command to bring back any gold and spoils.

He followed me to my tent and I gave him some water. "I've heard from the man you sent ahead about what took place back at their camp. You agree that they are a people of sorcery?" I asked him.

"My lord, they should all be put to death. We have no measure of their powers," he spat out of his bloodied mouth.

He was missing a few teeth, if I wasn't mistaken. All of this turmoil - for slaves!

"Tell me you found something worthwhile at their camp."

Nodding his head, he replied, "There was a golden case hidden in one of the tents. I dared not open it around the men or in the vicinity of that foul encampment. After what was unleashed on us, I am frightened that opening this case could release demons of unimaginable power."

Unhooking his mantle, he revealed an intricately carved golden chest that was the size of a coin chest. It was beautiful and would bring a profitable trade, but the carvings along the border could be evil. Or not. The Kahn could decide to open it.

"Good man. The Kahn will be pleased. I have tied up all the captives with their mouths securely fastened. I believe they speak their spells. We will cut their tongues out in the morning before we continue our journey home. Go get some rest. Daylight comes soon."

He bowed and then left my tent.

My curiosity had been piqued. There was one woman that would know about this case. After she had told me what was in it, I would cut her tongue out. There would be no more witchcraft and spells.

After a quick protection prayer to my ancestors, I marched outside to the slaves and brought Aigiarn back to my tent. I sat her down on the cushion as I sat on a cushion across from her.

"You have the case," she said somberly.

"I do. Tell me what it is and I will let you live."

"If I tell you what it is, you promise to not cut out my tongue?"

A mind reader and a witch. "You won't need your tongue as a slave."

She glared at me. "I offered you my body as a trade for my life. Now I offer you knowledge as a way for you to surpass even your Kahn. If you deny me, you will never be the leader of immeasurable power you were born to be."

Wow, I thought. She was good at saying what I wanted to hear.

"You don't have to believe me, Batuhan. I cannot breach your protections unless you invite me to. If you untie me, I will show you how to open the case."

I snorted. Not a chance that I would untie her. "I have decided to make you my concubine and you will bear me sons. If you please me tonight, Aigiarn, then maybe I will not remove your tongue in the morning."

Instead of looking alarmed as I had hoped she would, she smiled broadly showcasing very straight teeth. Her smile made her beautiful. "You've made a good bargain. I will show you the power you will have in this lifetime."

Lifting her from her cushion, I brought her on top of me as we fell back onto my cushion, letting her legs open to straddle my hips.

She was much smaller than my wife. I lifted up her skirts and ran my hands up her legs. She stared at me and smiled her encouragement. I did want to claim her as mine; she was captivating.

I untied my pants to unleash myself. Rubbing my shaft against her already moist lips, I saw her nod as she closed her eyes and moaned. I eased my hardness into her.

My mind kept repeating: I am the ultimate man, a warlord by nature, a conqueror of peoples, and a warrior with no scruples in killing whoever Genghis Kahn bade me to kill. Her wet tightness clenched my throbbing member. I moaned from the undeniable pleasure that coursed through my veins.

She started laughing and when I looked into her eyes, I saw the future. I saw myself sitting on the throne as the Kahn. Directing my people around me. She was sitting beside me with three boys at her feet. Our boys.

We were soaring above it all and flying in the clouds. I could feel the dampness of the air, felt the freedom offered by joining with her.

I kept thrusting, grasping her hips and slamming my aching hardness into her. I wanted to make her scream but she kept smiling and gazing deeply into my eyes.

"Keep going. This is only the beginning, Batuhan," she murmured close to my mouth right before she licked my bottom lip with her tongue.

I pulled her top down, exposing her breasts and suckled one nipple until she started grinding on top of me. She was moaning and crying. And clenching me tighter than I had ever felt before.

I threw her underneath me on the cushion and slammed into her, lifting her hips so my member penetrated her as deep as I could go. I wanted to punish her for being a witch, but she only lifted her hips higher in a welcome invitation.

"You're a greedy woman, aren't you, Aigiarn? I'm going to make you scream. I'm going to keep you pregnant all of the time so you will know that I am your lord."

"Yes, make me yours. Take me whenever and however you want me, my great Kahn," she moaned. She opened her eyes and held my gaze.

I pushed myself deeper and harder into her, knowing that I was going to come very soon. I watched her eyes dilate with her orgasm and her head fell back in breathless wonder. Her body was contracting around me and I could hold on no longer.

Buried to the hilt on top of her, I spilled my seed deep inside of her and she whispered in my ear, "It is done."

I could not move. I was drained completely.

Had she just claimed my soul? Was I now serving her?

What did I care; I saw what I would become with Aigiarn by my side. I would be the mightiest Kahn in history! I rolled over so she could get up and noticed her hands were still tied behind her back. She must be in pain, I thought.

As I watched her in amazement, she got on her knees and took my limpness into her mouth. She was sucking so intensely on me that I started to get hard again. She lifted her head, turned around and said over her shoulder, "Now, take me like a great Kahn, Batuhan."

Throwing her skirts up over her waist, I easily penetrated her from behind. I kept her hips in place with my hands and undoubtedly bruised her soft flesh. I pushed myself so deep inside, grinding into her until she screamed. I felt her pulsate around my hardened member and knew she was orgasming again. Then I emptied myself into her while she clenched my cock mercilessly, squeezing out every last drop of me into her womb.

At this rate, she would most certainly be pregnant this week.

"Will you untie me? At least one hand. I must clean myself," Aigiarn asked.

Knowing that a woman needed to clean herself or risk infection, I untied one of her hands while I kept the other grasped in my grip.

"You will trust me after I bear you your first son," she said. "There will be three and we will be happy. You will see, Batuhan. You will see."

That is what I had seen in the vision. But was it the future or was it something she had placed in my head because I was inside of her?

Turning from her, I let her go and went to grab the water bucket. "Here is some water. Wash yourself and then I must sleep. I will return you to the other women."

"If you return me now, it will look as if you refuse me. Keep me tied up but let me stay in your tent for the remaining hours until daybreak."

I took a moment to think on this.

"I will let you stay if you tell me what is in the golden case," I said, suddenly remembering the reason she was in my tent.

"There is a written secret in the case along with a few other sacred items used by our tribe. They remove us from trouble when the circumstances are dire and we face death."

"And these sacred items only work on your tribe? Or will they help others as well?" I asked.

Aigiarn's eyes gave nothing away as she replied, "They only work on our tribe as far as I know. Your men killed the master and he could have told you more. I have never seen the items nor the secret. Only the master could."

"Then I will open it. What is the trick?"

"Hold both of the far edges with your hands, and then place your thumbs on the upside-down masks. They should press inwards to pop the lid," she advised.

I did as she suggested but nothing happened.

"It's not working, witch." I glanced up at her to see Aigiarn examining the case closely. She was standing right next to me.

"Then you aren't pressing them in hard enough. Stretch your thumbs wider. Your thumbs must go completely into the case before the spring will open."

As I focused on the case and finished pushing my thumbs completely into the round holes, I felt a prick to my neck and dropped the case immediately.

"What…."I grabbed my neck as I fell on my knees. My blood was leaking out of me by the cup full.

"Goodbye, Oh Great Captor Batuhan. We will not meet again in this lifetime or the next. Our paths will cross in one more lifetime. Hopefully, you will be wiser."

She grabbed the case and silently ran out of the tent as I fell to the ground and watched the last of my blood gush out over my most treasured rug.

A few lessons learned in this lifetime:

When you are living in greed, power lust, murdering people (blood lust) and thriving off of the fear people have of you, there is a balance that must be kept and you will repeat this lesson over and over again. If, as an adult, you choose not to rise above your birth circumstances and you become a murdering psychopath like your father and his father before him, there are consequences that can include untimely death/murder and not seeing your children grow older, in this lifetime and the next. There is karmic reckoning.

Chapter 4

Queen Elizabeth's Court

❖

1579 CE

Queen Elizabeth reigned over Britain (and Ireland) in a show of strength and will. Due to scandal and the beheading of her mother, she kept her Boleyn relatives close and distant family ties even closer. Loyalty and trust were two very frail attributes in this time of power and greed, where strong women were brought down hastily and mercilessly.

I am from a royal bloodline. A cousin of the Queen, married to a Duke, dressed in the finery of my station. I want for nothing.

My every whim is usually met, unless it's my husband who's giving me something. Then, he plays his infantile games.

But I've already birthed the children. I've done my duty. The line was preserved. The boys had been sent from court to be raised on the dukedom lands. They must know their home and be safe from the intrigues of the court.

Four boys and one girl.

I was glad they were mostly boys; they would have the opportunities that I did not have. They would have the luxury of being freer to choose their path, although the eldest would have an arranged marriage as long as he lived when he was of age.

He could come to court once his marriage was arranged.

There is always something going on at court. I keep up with all of the alliances, dalliances and happenings but it is tiring sometimes. My husband's mistress is beautiful and keeps my husband from our loveless bed. This is marvelous considering that I am seeking the love of an attractive Italian Count. Lord knows if he was really a count. But he was so smooth and pleasing to look at. He could sing and dance with the best of them.

Whenever I see him, my heart flutters. I had to be careful of this growing love for him. I had sat on it for eight months, seeing if it would languish as most love affairs from afar tended to do at court. I had never been in love before. Yet here I am, still seeking him with my eyes as I walk into every room after eight months.

There is a small chance I will go to hell for not upholding my marriage vows. However, I had been married off young and I would not live that long, as not many women were known to reach old age after birthing five children.

I do not know how long I have to live. However, I am determined; I must have some love and fun in my life. After my boys had been sent off almost one year ago, there was less joy in my world. Certainly, there was much less love in it.

Now I am ready for love. I am older and wiser. I could keep the affair quiet, yet I knew that the Queen found out every little or big happening at her court. She enjoyed the collusions and tended to manipulate some of them when she was feeling bored.

How was a queen bored? I pondered. The wars seemed to never end. We are a violent country.

~~~

"Wife, we must talk," my husband yelled as he entered our chambers.

"Why, hello dear husband," I smiled at him coquettishly. Even though we were no longer lovers, I was fond of him as he had never mistreated me regardless of his childish games.

"My mistress wants more of my time. She wants to go away from court for a little while to visit my lands in the east. I would be gone for one month," he said, smiling back at me and looking to me for advice.

This is what our relationship was now. He looked at me for wisdom and I told him the truth in all matters, as much as was possible. His pride was easily wounded.

"One month? Could you shorten it to three weeks? The queen would not miss you as much from court if it was only three weeks. One month could lengthen to three fortnights which would prove disastrous. You know how she needs assurances and you are one of her unwavering supporters," I said casually.

"My dearest Anne, you are right, as always. There is continually something that must be done. I do not even know what my lands look like anymore, we have been so long at court. Did you wish to come as well?"

"Ha! That would be impossible. I have much to do here and our eldest will need to be betrothed soon. He is approaching ten years. The list of ladies suitable for his position grows shorter by the month. And we must align our family with someone similar to how we think. We can have no manipulations or schemes from her family," I said dispassionately.

My husband hated speaking about such things.

"I will heed your decision, my wife. You know best about such matters. Is there any way that you will be able to arrange all of this on your own, or will you need me?"

I smiled, "My dear, there is no need for you to arrange anything. I have everything covered. When do you leave?"

"We shall leave in three days' time. There is no need to delay. I will find the strength to be alone with my mistress for three entire weeks. Has it ever been done before?" he asked in such a sweet childish voice.

I laughed. I did not have the heart to tell him that this would lead to her wanting more from him. Mistresses at court perpetually wanted more. He would see that from her soon enough.

I replied, "You are a very courageous man. Let us hope she knows how blessed she is to have you as her lover."

He smiled broadly at that and bowed to me, then turned on his heels to rush back to his mistress with the news. It was nice to see him so happy; even if it would be short lived as all of his affairs were. He grew tired of the women when they asked for too much.

He was a family man, after all. His sons needed me, and he needed me. Our daughter was his secret joy, although he would never tell anyone but her that sentiment. I hope that when she is grown, she will find as much love with her husband as she has with her father, who has spoiled her terribly, or her life could turn out to be very dreary indeed.

There were so many loose ends to tie up here at court.

I had thought long and hard on whom would be the best betrothal for our son; who would be able to uphold the wealth and prestige that came with being one of us.

The demands would be massive and she would need to withstand pressure on all sides in order to serve our family and her husband, my firstborn.

Without being able to consult any confidante about such a young lady, I had only been able to watch and wait. Many parents spoke endlessly about how perfect their daughters were but after a little bit of digging, which mainly amounted to my trusted maid paying off their servants, the truth would come out that they either had no brains or were spoiled creatures used to having every whim obeyed.

My husband and I did not allow the random whipping of servants or slaves in any of our households or the trade of children as slaves, which seemed to be two favorite pastimes of many of the nobility.

Little by little, the eligible list for my eldest had dwindled to three young ladies under the age of fourteen. Heaven knew there was no way to do this based on looks or appeal. Taking stock of their parents only led to dismay. I held out hope that the girls would be lovely despite their parents or due to the more likely possibility that the mother had slept with a servant or lover and conceived in order to have a pretty child.

One could never be sure of these parental intrigues, and it hurt my head to even try to decipher the truth.

Perhaps I could beg the Queen for an audience and ask her what she thought. It might give her some relief to consider such a trifling matter as a betrothal, although it was a betrothal that would either uphold her position and her plans for the future of England or it could lead to her betrayal.

Yes, the Queen it is.

~~~

My maid returned an hour later with a reply from the Queen's secretary. She would see me in one hour in her chambers. I loved when I got to see her in her chambers versus the formal settings. She was so much funnier and human, and less worried about the entire world going up in flames without her control and direction.

After dressing myself carefully for my audience with her, for one should never outshine Queen Elizabeth in any way if one wished to keep in her good graces, I gracefully floated towards her chambers.

Her guards nodded at me. How they kept everyone's names straight in this infernal court was astonishing. I wondered if that was a question during the interview to become a guard.

"Can you memorize a person's name, face and their entire family along with all of their servants? Would you be able to memorize over 1,000 people's names, and those names and faces can change at the drop of a hat, along with their titles and residences?"

"Oh yes, that is what I have always wanted to be since I was a child; a person that guarded the queen with the extraordinary memory skills of a Priest or a monk," I thought.

I started to giggle at my own joke. Poor guards. They could lose their head if they let someone near the Queen that did not belong. Imposters, assassins, it did not matter. They had to keep her safe.

Walking inside her chamber, I curtsied lowly to Queen Elizabeth, who was seated on cushions with candles flickering and wine in goblets on the low table. Food was haphazardly placed around the area on golden plates.

"Hello, Duchess. Do sit down," the Queen smiled broadly as she gestured towards a few cushions across from her.

"Thank you for the audience in such a timely manner, my Queen. I thought it might take days before I could see you," I stated, smiling back at her.

"And miss a chance to discuss intrigue with my cousin? I have had enough of politics for today, possibly for an entire lifetime." She chortled at her own joke.

Her life was devoted to her country, her crown and her people. She was not getting out of politics until she died. But at least she was in good humor. This would be easier now. I could be open with her.

"I come before you for less of a court deception and more for your wisdom. You know that my eldest son is ten years of age now. I would have an alliance with a family that will support you and has supported you always, as we have."

"Is that all? A good match for your son? That should be simple, Anne," she declared as she brushed off an imaginary fleck from the front of her gown.

"I wish that it was that simple. You know the vast holdings of our family and the title that must be upheld. This girl cannot be simple or childish. She must be ready to lay down her life for her queen and her new family," I retorted.

She glanced up at me and stared me in the eyes. "Oh yes, I see. That leaves about what, two girls in the whole of England for your son to marry," she smartly replied with the edges of her mouth turning upwards.

I laughed. "There are three." I handed her the list as I tried not to make a face, but I knew that my face had screwed up into a tight frown. "Do you know any of them? Their parents are all quite… hmmm…what's the word?"

She barked out, "Terrifyingly ugly?"

I could not contain my snort of laughter and our combined mirth startled her maids. Both of us took a few minutes to catch our breath.

"My Queen, I would not want the marriage to be doomed from the beginning. You know how hard it is at court with all of the mistresses and lovers taken. I wish to preserve some form of marriage vows for them as a young couple without him praying every night to God due to a disagreeable wife."

"I understand, my dear," and she patted my hand. "There is nothing that would give me greater pleasure than to arrange this for you, Anne. I can have paintings of the girls brought from their houses in the guise of picking the fairest daughter in the land to serve as one of my maids. All nonsense of course, but it might be useful to train her here before she is set off into the wilds of running massive manors, and a husband."

"As always, your insight is the best guidance that I could ask for. Thank you so very much."

"Does your husband know you are arranging this," she queried.

"He has left it in my hands. You know that he wants nothing to do with arranged marriages and the next generation. He's too vain for that. He will never grow old, or so he imagines." I winked at her.

"You are quite happy, are you not, my dear cousin? Is your marriage so bad? I know about your arrangement but I had hoped you, at the very least, have some sort of solace."

I cocked one side of my mouth up into the hint of a smile. "I do not have a lover, if that is what you are enquiring about. I had hoped for one years ago. Perhaps a true love of sorts or at least something romantic. My husband is quite a nice fellow but we spend very little time together, as you know. Since the children are all away, I have found more time to ponder my desires and I have found I am simply craving some love and tenderness from a man that adores me. But is such a thing truly possible?"

The thoughtful look on the Queen's face let me know she was contemplating the truth of sincere love. I knew the rumors of her youth and of her true love, as some people called him. In positions of such power, was true love ever allowed, especially as a woman?

Maybe one of my five children could marry for love. I am hopeful that it could be so.

She let out a lengthy sigh before she responded. "The answer to such a question is surely different for every individual. A man might claim he is in love with a woman however he will tire of her and move on within a year. A woman will die from a broken heart before anybody can tell what ails her, all due to the actions of a lover spurning her. I do hope that you find a bit of love in this place, my cousin. There is no shortage of charming men at court and you are still young. Enjoy yourself for once instead of being so responsible. Life is short."

I was astounded. Life was indeed short. Who knew how much longer I would live?

"You are right, my Queen. There is no guarantee. Thank you."

"Now leave your son's betrothal to me. Once the paintings are sent over, I will call you here to view them. You might want to start praying for some semblance of beauty now," she chuckled softly.

"Oh, I will immediately start my prayers. I look forward to our next meeting, my Queen." I stood and curtsied.

She nodded her head at me in dismissal and turned to speak with one of her maids.

~~~

There was no guarantee on how long we would live, I thought stoically as I eyed the scene before me.

It was the after dinner entertainment; dancing, singing, stories recited, people conversing about serious issues or gossiping about the happenings in foreign courts; everyone enjoying this small period of time before the betrayals and back stabbing started afresh in the morning.

Dressed in my finest evening dress, which was not my favorite dress but a close second, I drew the admiring gaze of many men. The dress was a bit low cut, but nothing unusual for the times, and the dark blue color enhanced my coloring and assets in a beautiful and sensual manner. The silk shaped my body as if it had been poured over my skin, and I knew that the top parts of my milky breasts were enticing along with my beautifully shaped neck.

As far as bodies went, I was very blessed compared to some that walked around this court. Not enough mixing of the bloodlines was a widespread issue since many of the mothers and fathers found it distasteful to marry their children off to people outside of their 'pure' blood. It also helped ensure titles and lands did not leave their families. However, it made for some very disfigured and distasteful looking people.

Speaking of families, my husband was nowhere to be seen in the crowded room although he had been at the dinner, smiling and flirting his way through every course.

There was a sense of longing and freedom in the air, as if the night stood still in order for lovers to achieve their secret trysts.

It was time I found the Italian Count. Life was short, after all. I could feel my death coming closer but I did not know when it would be. Hopefully after my son's marriage.

No matter, I was on a mission to have one night of love making. Everything else could wait. Tonight I would put my needs first.

Making my way to the refreshment table, I ordered a glass of wine. It was a liberty I rarely indulged in since the night I had drank too much of it and paid the price the following day. It surely was poison for the system if it could leave a person feeling so wretched and depressed in its aftermath.

Slowly turning from the table, I saw that he was standing right before me.

"Duchess Anne, you are looking ravishing this evening," he proclaimed as he kissed my hand gallantly and proceeded to elegantly bow over it.

The sparkle in his eye told me all I needed to know. He appreciated my figure, my beauty and my dress.

"You are very kind, dear Count. Tell me, are you enjoying this lovely evening?" I asked him with eyebrows slightly raised.

One could never tell with a flirt, and Italian men were known for being quite the flirts as well as very passionate lovers.

"I was merely entertained by this evening until I happened upon your glorious being. Now I am enchanted," he quipped back at me, an arrogant yet sheepish smile upon his handsome face.

This could go on all night.

I smiled back at him, wondering if he knew how much I wanted him.

"My lady, would you dance with me? I have not had the honor of dancing with the most beautiful woman at this English Court since I arrived here."

I giggled. "You, sir, are a horrible flirt. I am sure you say that to all of the ladies."

His features contorted into mock astonishment followed by pain. "My dearest lady, you wound me. I profess my admiration for your beauty and consequently you laugh at me."

He held out his hand to lead me onto the dance floor. Placing my hand in his, he wasted no time in sweeping me into his arms and waltzing with me around the dance floor. We whirled past the other couples in a dizzying display of silks and finery, beauty and manliness.

There was a time that I would have cared that he held me a bit too close and brushed my body with his body every now and then.

Tonight was unlike the other nights though. My responsibilities and cares were left for tomorrow.

Whispering into my ear, with his tongue slightly touching the lobe, his accent stirring my passion even further, he added fuel to the flames. "You know that I have been waiting for you to come to me, to allow me to love you, and here you are. Allowing me to dance with you and hold you close. I must be in heaven," he sighed.

His face was close to mine and I could have kissed him. But I would never cause a scene in a public place; it was against my breeding.

Everyone at this court might take lovers and parade them around, yet my breeding and my connection to the queen prevented even the slightest hint of indecency on my part. I was simply a woman. If I had been a man, it might have been different.

"Would you enjoy dancing with me regularly, my dear count?" I probed.

His face lit up into an unabashed smile. "That would give me great pleasure, my lady."

"I cannot promise to always dance with you. However, I will dance with you as much as is respectable without calling undue attention to our persons. You know my position in this court."

He nodded his head and a few dark black locks of hair fell out of place, making him look younger than I had thought him to be.

"How old are you, count?"

"Oh, that is not polite. I have not asked you your age. But I will tell you regardless. I am twenty-two," he boldly stated, ignorant or uncaring to the fact that I am quite a few years older than he.

"And do you have a penchant for older women," I teased.

The Count laughed as he continued to twirl me about the dance floor. "I only have a penchant for one woman and she is in my arms this very instant."

He really was a flirt, albeit a most deliciously handsome and charming one.

There was a possibility that I could deeply fall for him, if he did not remind me of my husband at that age. Although he was more strikingly attractive and appealing than my husband had ever been, there was something about him that was almost dangerous and deceptive at the same moment.

I could ponder this later. Right now, I would relish in this flirting and what would come of it. He would be in my bed this night; I knew this in my bosom.

"Dear count, is your bedroom very big and beautiful? Mine has a lovely view of the gardens and is quite large." Dear god, I had well-nigh invited him to my rooms or me to his rooms. This was a first for me.

His steps faltered for one second then he resumed the dance with poise. He stared down at me intently as I smiled up at him timidly.

"No, my lady. My rooms are not as beautiful as yours are. However, the privacy of my rooms, as they are on a different floor than all of the other lords and ladies, is quite worthwhile."

"Quite worthwhile?" I questioned him.

"Yes. If you happen to be loud in the bedroom, my lady," he responded to me with a massive smile.

I could feel my face flushing. How did I know if I was loud while love making? I had only ever had it with my husband to produce heirs, never for fun and definitely not for my moaning or pleasure. Making love to my husband currently would be akin to being with a best friend or family member; that is how much our relationship was an alliance not based upon love.

I pondered on my moaning and I wondered if he would enjoy my sounds of ecstasy.

The heat was getting to be a bit much for me, as it was traveling up from my pelvis to my head and my breathing became heavier. I licked my lips for some moisture.

He stared down at my lips and grasped me tighter against his body. I could feel him hardening against my stomach.

"My lady, I would be honored to escort you to the garden for some air. You look a bit flushed," he encouraged.

"Yes, the garden would be nice," I replied, hoping some air might calm my heart rate down. He was very exciting.

Escorting me out onto the terrace and down the steps to the garden, I knew what the love stories meant when they spoke of hearts beating out of their chests and fairy tales. Being in his presence was making me forget that I was married. Spending an hour with him might lead to all manners of follies dancing around in my head.

Yet I knew there was no going backwards. I would accept his love this night and take what I could get. My life had been wasted emotionally; everything was stifled under duty and family, although my children gave me great joy when I was permitted to be around them. I did miss them terribly.

But tonight was for me, and only me.

After we had walked a bit into the garden, he led me to a secluded bench where we would be sheltered from any others taking air in the garden. Nobody would see us.

He looked down at me and smiled. "Anne? Might I call you Anne? I am going to kiss you now," he whispered as he pressed his lips against mine without waiting for an answer.

His lips were so soft and demanding, while one of his hands drew my waist closer against his body. I opened my mouth on a moan and he slid his tongue slowly inside, teasing my tongue to play with his.

Our breathing melded together and I could feel his heart hammering against my chest.

Breaking away from our kiss, he murmured, "Darling, I must have you. Do you want me?"

"You know that I do."

"Then let us be off to my room. The door locks and we can be alone and unbothered. Please say yes, dearest Anne," he ended with a sigh.

Nodding yes, I grabbed his hand and he led me to a side entrance slightly beyond the garden. Checking to ensure we were not seen, he would leave me in the shadows and confirm that each hallway or stairway was empty before leading the way.

His gentle urging and pulling was all I needed. I could not be with him if he were forceful or a brute. I needed tender love and sweetness. My body was craving this as well.

After what seemed like an eternity, we arrived at his door. He guided me inside and I noticed the fire was already lit. His rooms seemed cozy and warm, similar to him.

With a smile, he turned back to the door and turned the key in the lock. "Now we are safe," he said laughingly.

He understood the delicacy of the situation and I knew that I was protected. Although I would not be able to make a habit of this wonderful evening, I knew there would be no whispers about it throughout court tomorrow as there had been for so many others.

Coming to a standstill directly in front of me, he pulled me towards the fire and began kissing me again. This time, he was kissing my neck and the tops of my breasts, forcing me to lean my head back and expose more of my naked flesh to him.

"Amore Mia, I must remove your dress. I cannot wait another moment," he huskily revealed.

I could feel his excitement and rejoiced in it. The feeling of being seduced is rather heady, I discovered in that moment. He could do anything he wanted to me and I would say yes. Or nod yes, as I was beyond speaking at this point.

His hands were everywhere at once. I could feel him undoing all of the buttons on my dress with one hand and the other hand playing with a nipple. He had pressed his hard member into my behind, and was rubbing against me as he pulled my dress down my shoulders and past my waist. I stepped out of my dress as he guided me to, and he placed my dress neatly upon a chair so it would not get wrinkled.

Unlacing my corset, he started to yank it down so that his hands had full access to my breasts. He started pulling on my nipples and my knees went weak. It was pleasure and pain at the same time. A ball of pleasure was forming in my stomach and spreading throughout my body.

Turning me around, he tugged my undergarments off my body in a very adept manner, throwing them aside. I was completely bare before him.

Before I could contemplate getting his clothes off of him, he leaned down and started sucking on my right nipple. His left arm went behind me, making my back arch and pushing my womanhood towards him. With his right hand, he started to gently feel past my curls and into my moist folds, seeking my heated center.

"Oh, you are dripping wet, Cara Mia."

He picked me up and carried me to the bed. "Open your legs for me, Anne" he demanded.

I obeyed; he immediately buried his head in between my legs, sucking and teasing as his fingers stoked me into a frenzy.

My moans were loud and my breathing started to quicken. "Yes, let it happen. Let me give you full pleasure, Amore Mia."

As he said that, he pinched one of my nipples with his fingers while his tongue continued its assault upon my pleasure point. His other fingers were going in and out of me at a rapid pace and my hips were keeping time with him.

I whispered, "Oh my god," as I felt the pleasure burst, resembling a million stars shooting throughout my entire body. I started shaking and I felt myself clench his fingers, pulling them deeper up into me.

Without losing a second, he thrust his unleashed manhood into me, covering me with his body and bringing the feelings back again into the base of my stomach.

He was so long and thick, I thought, as I began to convulse around his thrusts. I was going to reach the point again, simply with his thrusting going in and out of me. I felt like I was on fire.

My head fell back as I lost control and my sight went black after the starburst of gold as I experienced my pleasure yet again.

"Yes, this is what I wanted. Let it happen again, Anne. Another time," he breathed into my ear as he kept pounding away.

He lifted my hips, really diving deeply into me, until I felt that he was hitting my stomach. He was hitting something. But it felt divine. This was what made women go insane; this pleasure. Once you have felt it, you don't ever want to let it go.

As he grabbed my behind even harder, pulling me in closer to him, I could feel the sweat between us, making our bodies' slick. The pounding sound started to come faster and faster, and I knew I would have bruises on my derriere and inner thighs tomorrow.

I could feel my body tighten around him, and I knew another time was coming. He felt it also and moaned but kept going. He was a man on a mission.

Losing myself in the pounding and pleasure, I felt my body turn to mush. I could not even keep my arms around him and they dropped to the bed.

He smiled and said, "One more time, Amore Mia."

"Are you trying to kill me? I cannot feel my legs or my arms," I sighed. I could not even speak.

"Four times and I will stop. I promise."

Continuing his thrusts deep into me, I could feel the ball of pleasure start to gather again. It was much quicker each time, as if my body anticipated his need to keep going and wanted to please him.

My breathing was almost as labored as his and I could tell he was trying hard not to finish.

"Tell me you are going to finish. It will excite me more," I murmured against his throat where I had been kissing his neck.

His body tensed up and I could feel his internal fight for control.

"I'm going to release my seed soon, Amore Mia. I'm going to push it so deep up into your belly that you will never forget this night and you will never forget who pleasured you so thoroughly or so many times. I'm going to hammer my seed up into you until you scream my name, Anne."

Those words did it. That pushed me over the edge. "Yes, oh my god, yes, please give it to me. Please," I begged while he hammered into me so hard that I thought the massive wooden bed was going to break. My body convulsed and my eyelids closed, feeling it more intensely and throbbing everywhere, as if my body was physically pulsing.

He started to moan and thrust harder, "Yes, yes, here I go, so deep up inside of you. Yes. Yes. Yes."

His warmth poured into me while he kept pumping deeper, as if to shove his seed further into my womb. Finally stilling, he was sheathed all of the way inside of me and I could feel a bit more of his seed come out.

Then he gently removed himself from me and fell exhausted onto the bed.

"I will not be able to move for a while," I whispered to his back as he was lying face down on the bed.

Turning his head towards me and grinning, he responded, "There is no need to go anywhere until close to dawn. I will wake you up, Anne. Rest now beside me as I rest with you."

After pulling the covers up over both of us, he gathered me into his arms and promptly fell asleep. I lay there with my eyes closed, marveling at the beauty of this night. My whole body thrummed with bliss and gratification.

I fell asleep peacefully and soundly.

~~~

I was awakened by him rubbing himself against my behind while one hand tugged on my nipple. It had to be only a few hours since we had made love, if even that.

My wetness started between my legs as he continued to pull and tease my nipples and I ground my behind into his hardened member to let him know that I was awake and willing.

He chuckled into my ear before he started to kiss my neck. Not waiting to even check if I was wet, he parted my folds and plunged himself deep inside of me.

Whimpering, I could feel the intensity rising. I wanted more.

Somehow, he must have known this as he shoved me onto my belly and continued driving his hardness into me. There was no gentleness this time, only possessive taking. I could tell he was about to release his seed into me again.

Instead, he pulled out and spun me over onto my back.

Thrusting into me even harder, he started to get a bit rougher. "Do you like this? How hard I am taking you? Do you feel that you have no control?"

"Yes, oh yes. Don't stop. Please."

"Oh, I'm not going to stop. Not yet."

As the pounding was unrelenting, I peaked and on a moan, released even more wetness between my legs.

He looked surprised but he kept going.

Bringing his hands up to my throat, he lightly squeezed to see what I thought. It made me clench him even tighter and he moaned.

The pressure around my neck increased until I came again, and I could feel him start releasing himself inside of me. And similar to the first time, he kept pounding deeper and deeper up into me.

However, his hands kept getting tighter and tighter around my neck.

I tried to grip his hands with my hands and let him know to stop. His eyes were darker now and no sound was coming out of my mouth. His hands were too tightly wrapped around my throat.

I could feel him inside of me as he kept choking me.

Thoughts raced through my head: Oh God, he was strangling me. I have to fight. I have to live. I must get out from under him. Escape his grip. I cannot die like this. My eldest son. The Queen. What would happen to my children?

I started to kick my legs and try to move but he held me pinned under him with his entire weight upon my body.

But it was too late. I had no more air. Everything went black.

~~~

What a horrible, yet memorable, way to die.

Looking down at my lifeless body on the bed, I realized that strangulation might be the quickest death and a one night stand was no replacement for love, no matter how lonely I felt in my marriage.

A few lessons learned in this lifetime:

When you accept the social norms, for example putting up with a husband's cheating because that is what everyone else in your circle does, your life becomes empty and loveless. There's a whole world beyond doing what is expected of you and people pleasing, and when you fall in line with everyone else, you abandon your true self and have no self-worth which leads to fleeting (if any) fulfilment of your desire to be loved.

Chapter 5

Native American Daughter

❖

1835 CE

The United States was spreading west as land was forcefully taken by the government and wealthy landowners. Despite the peaceful and helpful ways of 98% of the East Coast Native American tribes (warring tribes existed in the West), the government did not want to work with or have Natives mixing in their towns and cities. Thus, tribes were brutally murdered and wiped off the face of the earth in the quest for empire expansion. The Trail of Tears was a series of the government's forced relocation programs of Native Americans that spanned decades and over one thousand miles, where the number of Natives killed remains unknown.

Her life was very calm and peaceful, and she gave thanks to the Great Spirit for that.

From a young age, she felt different than other girls. She was always running around, trying to learn as much as she could about everything, as long as her mother did not catch her.

Her mother was very cold and proud. She had an idea of how her daughter's life should be and it was not as a medicine woman. As a young girl, she would sneak into the Medicine Man's teepee and learn as much as she could without getting caught. Her best friend would always say she was with him, if her mother ever asked.

She could not understand why her mother said no to everything that her spirit wanted. Her spirit yearned to heal people and to spend time in nature. But her mother, Agasga, wanted her to learn to cook, clean hides, make clothes, and know all of the essentials of how to be a good wife.

There was no desire in her to have children or a husband. If she had to marry, she would marry her best friend and that would be comparable to marrying her brother, but it would be better than marrying someone she did not know or love.

Yet, she knew her father would never make her marry. He had not agreed to anything her mother spoke of, nor would he force her to do something she was so against. Her father was her biggest ally besides her grandpa.

Oh, her grandpa. All of his stories about wild animals and horses. He had been a legend in his youth. He had tamed wild horses easily and wild animals would follow him around. He once had a pet wolf and a pet mountain lion. Now, he sat and told stories and watched her younger brother, Adohi, who was ten years younger than she was. Her mother's pride and true love was seen only for Adohi.

Sometimes she wondered if Agasga truly was her mother because she seemed to hate her most of the time. There was no connection between them, no spirit binding them as most families were bound in her tribe. Her mother's touch was alien to her, as she was not touched very often by Agasga. Even her name, Agasga, meant rain; as if Agasga was only here to make her cry.

This was not something that bothered her. Her grandpa and father more than made up for the loss of love between her and her mother.

They knew she felt more like a man. She was one of the two-spirited people – a man in a woman's body. And her mother refused to accept or allow it, as if she could stop it using her denial of it.

She used to run around with no shirt on and buckskin pants she had borrowed from her best friend, dressed as a boy while they played the hunting game in the woods. They would be out all day, chasing each other, building huts to hide in, trying to catch animals for their supper.

Eventually, Agasga made her give that up after she caught her with no shirt on, running around wildly in the woods. Her mother had screamed at her and pointed at her chest. Looking down, the girl finally saw that she was growing breasts.

That had been many moons ago. There was no running around anymore. She had to be serious and know her place, to act like a woman so that she would get a good man to marry her.

But what was her place?

Her father would always let her go with him to meet the traders. Their tribe traded furs and hides in a white trading camp. This was the new way of their world, and the trades were good for her people. Most of the traders were respectful and curious about their way of life. Their language was strange but easy for her to learn. She never spoke to them, however she learned their words. Her mind was like the ground that soaked up the rain after many dry weeks.

The excitement she felt when in the trading camp helped her know that she would lead a different life. It was not normal for her to be around so many men, but her father let her dress as a man and referred to her as his son. She was large for a woman and her breasts were small enough to not stand out. The traders knew she would carry on the trading after her father became too old. But that would not be for many years.

Disapproval was all she received from her mother after she would accompany her father on these trading visits. Usually, this meant Agasga would not speak to her for a few days, which was not a hardship for either of them it seemed. Her grandfather would laugh and ask her what she had learned in the trading village. She would always pick up a new word or two, and he would practice with her since he was the first one to have learned the white man's language long ago.

Why was her mother so backwards? The times were changing; the land was becoming more populated. More traders and their families were coming. Agasga must see her worth as the one to follow in her father's footsteps.

She was also good with a bow and arrow, and her father was teaching her to shoot the rifle they had received as a gift from his old trading friend, Michael. Michael was from a far-off island called Ireland and he had red hair that was going white. He preferred to live as they did, roaming the land in a buckskin tent he could put behind him on the saddle of his horse. He always gave her a new treat from a vast town of white people he visited every few months. His tales of how large the other white settlements were growing made her eyes widen and her father would become silent with a sad look on his face.

Their ways and culture were the bonds that made her people strong. If the land kept getting swallowed up by farms and white people, they would have to seek land in unknown places, far away from where their people had lived for hundreds of years.

She knew enough to know that everything changes; weather, land, animals, everything. All people must bend and grow. One old tribe from far up north still spoke of a great flood that killed everything and everyone except those that had built very large canoes. The few from their tribe that had survived had to regrow their food and rebuild their tribe after the flood went away. But that was from the time before the moon, the time the elders rarely spoke of anymore.

Even though that flood was long ago, that story felt similar to the flood of white people now washing over the land. This storm would have no mercy.

There was nothing that could be done to stop the white people from coming. There were so many of them, and they all had guns. Most stories were of how they would kill first, and then become peaceful after, similar to a few warring tribes that she had heard of but thankfully had never run into.

Her grandpa would ask her about the trading town, if it was larger, what all was being traded, and if there were soldiers. She kept very good notes in her head for him and she knew this was spoken about around the council fire. Decisions would be made to protect their people. The land belonged to nobody, but it was time for their people to move to protect their ways.

"Sitting Bear, come here for a moment," her grandpa asked her. He had given her this nickname when she was four years old because she would sit and watch him for hours on end before falling asleep, similar to a hibernating bear. He was the only person she knew who had ever seen or been close to a hibernating bear in its cave.

"You must tell me what you saw in the trading camp. What were the people wearing? Were there more buildings?"

"Yes, grandfather. There were many new people and buildings. One was called a mercantile and had hats in the windows. The other was called a church with a wooden shape like this," and she made a 't' with her arms. "The church is where they go on Sundays to pray while a man screams at them about hell and fire and death. It is a very unhappy way to spend a few hours of your life each week."

"Ah, yes. Their religion has come. This is now going to be a large town in a few years' time," he stated, knowing that the tribe would have to move sooner than he thought. A church going up meant it was safe for families and new people to come. The town lines would grow further into their homeland, and more farmers would come to clear trees and grow crops. Trade would continue and prosper, but their tribe must find a new home.

She hoped with the new beginnings that her mother would allow her to be who she wanted to be. She was now twenty-five.

Noticeably, Sitting Bear was too old to marry, although Agasga would mention names of young men that were available in the tribe. Truthfully, her mother's last hope had died when Sitting Bear's best friend had married a young woman, instead of her, five years ago.

They had tried to kiss when they were eighteen. She wanted to know what it felt like and if anything would spark inside of her. He had agreed, which only showed her that she liked women and not men, something they both knew and had spoken about although it remained unspoken of in her family. This first kiss was a learning experience for Sitting Bear, in many ways.

He spat afterwards, said it was like kissing his sister and he claimed he would never kiss her again. They laughed and knew then that they were the best of friends. They understood each other so well.

Years later, it was she that pointed out his future wife to him when he did not see the young woman's flirtatious manner towards him. His marriage to this woman was beautiful. Their children were considered as her nephews and she knew that their next child would be a girl. It was one of Sitting Bear's gifts.

She knew that she would never have children nor did she wish to. It was a long painful process that her body did not desire to have. And that was fine with her since she had a brother who would be married off soon. Agasga was parading women in front of him now that Adohi had turned fifteen. He was still young in Sitting Bear's opinion, but their mother would not hear of waiting. Someone had to give her grandchildren and marry to carry on the bloodline, Agasga would say as she glared at Sitting Bear.

Her brother had grown into a fine young man. Sitting Bear was very protective over Adohi and helped him learn as much as she could. Their connection was strong and he looked up to her for guidance. She was teaching Adohi the white man's language because he would help her with the trading when their father decided it was time. Only the Great Spirit knew when that time would be, she decided as she looked off into the glorious woods. Her brother's name, Adohi, meant 'woods'.

~~~

It had been decided. The council decreed that we would move after the fall harvest of corn; that we could no longer wait another year.

They made offerings and danced to thank Mother Earth for her bounty and blessings they had received in this beautiful land, for all of the years of support and nourishment, love and peace that the tribe had maintained. The dancing was beautiful, and the drumming thundered into her heart making her feel as one with the earth, Great Spirit and the Celestial Star Family - above and always.

She would be sad to leave this home land, the only place she had ever known. Yet she was excited to see a new place. Life was changing and nobody could stop it. No amount of prayers to the Great Spirit would keep them in this land. The new wave of darkness in the fleshy reality had become clear. In her heart, she took a deliberate, sacred moment to think of her ancestors and still find something to be thankful for.

Their father and a few of the other men had gathered up the last of their hides and furs yesterday to trade in the neighboring town where they usually traded. This would be the last trade until they had settled onto their new land. Once the trading men returned two days later, the tribe would be on its way to the new unknown territory that would be their home.

The scouts had found their new home after speaking with a few other friendly tribes. It was four days of riding on horseback from their old land which could mean a week or so of travel, depending on how fast they could move the young and the elderly. There were not enough horses for everyone.

After many meetings with the council about the land - what it looked like, who their new neighbors were, and how near to water they would be – they had agreed to this new place. One week of travel would reveal an entirely new world to her and their tribe.

~~~

As they continued to pack and prepare the tribe for moving, she felt her fear increase. Her father had not returned and it was the third day. He should have returned the evening before. Some of their tribe had left the previous day. These families had their food and clothing supplies set on the horses, ready to go, awaiting the rally. She wished she was one of them.

Something was wrong. She could feel it but did not know what it was. She was not a healer who had visions like the medicine man did but Sitting Bear had very strong intuition.

There was a chill in the wind. The trees seemed to whisper. Staring harder at them, she heard them say, "Run."

Run? Where did that come from? Was it a warning? Did she have the gift of visions? She was confused by her thoughts. She started to run towards the Medicine Man and ask him what he felt.

Upon entering the Medicine Man's teepee, she felt a different energy. It moved and reshaped itself. She saw the old man sitting by his animal skins on the ground. He had not packed at all.

Where was his helper?

"Wise one, what is this? What is this feeling? Something is not right," she breathlessly murmured.

"They are coming," he stated, gazing at his fire.

"Who?"

"The white men on horses. They do not come in peace. You must tell the council. Now. Go," he said as he urged her out of his teepee with his eyes. He had not moved from his seat.

She ran towards the chief's tent. The council was spread out. The chief would need to know first.

Too many people were walking about.

Where were the scouts? Why was the alarm not raised?

Shouting as she ran, the chief heard her loud cry and came out of his tent with his widened eyes showing alarm. Nobody had ever heard her war cry. People were following her to understand what was going on.

As she halted in front of her chief, she blurted out, "The wise one said the white men on horses are almost here. They do not come in peace."

"We must leave now. Abandon anything that is not packed," he commanded, looking around the circle of gathered tribal members. The group dispersed quickly.

Running to her teepee, she yelled for her brother. Adohi came rushing to her. "You must not leave my side. Whatever happens, we stay together." He nodded his head.

They had tied what they could to their horse. Grandfather, her mother, her brother and she rushed towards the north edge of the camp, the direction the tribe was to leave from.

~~~

It was time.

The chief nodded as all who could travel had arrived. They started their march.

What a poor-looking group they made; very few men with mostly women and children. They would be unable to defend themselves properly if attacked. She had counted their numbers. Less than fifty of her people remained.

Their scouts were missing. She had to think they were killed by the white men because they would never abandon their tribe. The scouts, at least, would have added a bit of strength to their numbers.

Where was her father? Hopefully, Michael had hidden him if something bad had happened in the trade town. Holding out for that hope would help her focus on leading her family to safety.

When they reached the first wooded hill beyond the camp, she turned around and looked.

The teepees that were still standing contained some of their elders. The ones who refused to slow them down so that they could escape the wrath and brutality of the white men; some were elders who were unable to move without being carried.

The Medicine Man had stayed behind as well. His time was near, he had proclaimed. He was from a long line of great visitors, those that could walk in both worlds and spoke to other great visitors. The stories passed down from the tribe's ancient ones spoke of the foreign race that was called forth to help his people and cast spells; the tall race of visitors.

That was the energy she had felt in his teepee; the hidden ways from a time before the great flood that she had never gotten to learn from the wrinkled and wise medicine man.

He had called on the tall visitors to help their people.

While the old men and old women, those that had stayed behind to guard his teepee, the Medicine Man sent out the curse. He cursed the white soldiers coming to kill his tribe. He cursed their families and homes, and any children they had or would have.

He called upon the energy of the tall ancient visitors to enact similar death and destruction on them, the horrifying annihilation that would happen to his tribe today, upon the bloodlines of the white soldiers.

As the old men and women chanted and their energy rose to the sky, the old Medicine Man lifted his hands into the air and sang the old words that would bind the curse to the white men and be unbreakable for the next seven generations of their bloodlines.

He sang out one long, powerful, rumbling cry, "Ah-yosh-sha-ta-me, aya-ki-yosh sha-ta-me," and picked up his knife and sliced his hand, pouring his blood onto the earth next to the fire and then on top of the fire where it sizzled. The elders outside of his teepee sliced their hands as well, turning their bloody hand towards the ground as they marched boldly around the teepee in a circle.

The Medicine Man stared up at the tall visitor that only he could see inside of his teepee, as the visitor nodded his head in acknowledgement and then vanished. It was done. There would be retribution for the violence that would be carried out today towards his tribe.

The white soldiers had no idea that they would be the recipients of a generational curse that would cause their sons and grandsons and great-grandsons to roil in self-inflicted pain, sorrow, trauma and despair, suicide and violence.

There would be balance. The Medicine Man smiled at the white men that came through his teepee and remained smiling as they shot him to death.

~~~

Sitting Bear and Adohi continued the trek, looking back from time to time to see if they were being followed. They were going at a steady pace but making too many tracks for the white men to follow. This was not good.

She said a quick prayer to Mother Earth for rain or an early snow; anything to hide their progress that marked the ground. Her tribe needed the earth's help.

The woods continued to shield their march, which was taking them further away from their home. They could do this. Perhaps the troops would not find them. After all, how many of them could there be? Five or ten?

They had not heard any cries or yells coming from their old home. Maybe the troops had turned away or decided not to kill the elders. Maybe they were after something else instead of her people.

Praying for protection from the Great Spirit, she plodded along following the others. Their footsteps fell quietly on the ground.

That's when she heard it. The first boom of a gunshot; a chilling sound that can never be mistaken for anything else.

Glancing around, she saw an elder man fly off the lead horse and land on the ground. They were no match for rifles. Their guns had gone with the scouts and her father's men, none of whom had caught up to them yet.

She grabbed her brother's arm and pulled him to the ground. Who knew how many guns they had?

The firing continued for what seemed like an eternity. Women and men fell to the ground all around them. A wail had risen up from the massacre that was even louder than the gunfire. She could see many others had taken cover on the ground. Most of the horses had either run away or been killed as well.

Why was this happening? Her tribe was a peaceful people. They were leaving their land so the white people could take it. Why couldn't they just let them go?

Her brother started to shake. The fear coursing through his veins had made his body react. She put her hand over his mouth to keep him silent and to tell him she was with him. Adohi was squeezing his eyes shut.

She did not know how long they laid there. Maybe the white men would think they were all dead and just leave.

But there was never any chance of that. They walked by each body on the ground and kicked it. The sounds varied; from screams, breaths being knocked out of lungs, and the crunching of bones being broken, to children sobbing and women crying.

"Enough. We march them north. To their new land. Let's get them up without killing them all. We promised the general we would deliver them to their land," she heard a man holler. He must be the leader.

What land? North how far? How many members of her tribe were left?

Her foot was kicked and her head jerked around to see the person responsible. One of the men motioned for her to come. She grabbed her brother and hauled him up with her.

The remainder of her tribe gathered together, terror and pain on every face. They could not speak the white man's language.

"They are taking us north to some new land. Their commander told them to take us there," she reassured them confidently. Their eyes looked at her and they nodded their acceptance. With panic written all over their faces, they seized as many of their belongings as they could.

A man walked swiftly up to Sitting Bear and punched her in the stomach. She staggered backwards, gasping for air while she tried to stay upright. Her brother was about to react but she motioned to him to stay still.

She regained her breath and said to the man that had punched her, "We are not your enemy. We are moving to new land away from here. Let us go. You will never see us again."

All of the white men stared at her with alternating looks of disgust, hatred and amusement.

The man who had punched her backed away from her as if she were a bear, while the leader rode his horse right up next to her.

"Oh, this one can speak English? Then you will know we can kill you easily. You are heading up north. We do not care about your plans. You are going to live where the General of the Army says you will live," he said.

Defiantly, she raised her chin. "We have never broken our word. We give you our word that we will never be seen in this land again. We are moving far away from here. There is no need for murder."

The leader sneered at her, reminding her of the story Michael had told her regarding a fire in the trading village that had been started by the white army. They had wanted a specific plot of land for a government building and the owner had refused to sell it to them. The fire had suspiciously started on the roof of the owner's building, which was a blacksmith in the front, and he had lived in the back with his family. The family had all been burned alive.

There had been other stories about the white army's ruthless ways and 'conquer all, kill all' mentality. They did not care who they murdered, friend or foe, woman or child; all in the name of gathering more land and riches, religion or government. It all boiled down to ownership and greed – because there truly was plenty of land to go around.

"You will go where we take you, if you make it. If you all die, it's less for us to worry about. Now move," the leader ordered.

His troops started pushing her people forward with their rifles to start them marching. She grasped her brother's arm, along with a few of their packed belongings which were scattered on the ground, and started following the guard who was leading.

She tried not to look down, not to see all of the dead faces on the ground, staring in horror at the sky. But she saw a few; the chief, his wife, and all of the men.

Her grandpa?! She wildly swung her head, searching for him. No, she thought. He would never make the march. He was so old now, she thought as tears threatened to spill onto her cheeks. She would not cry in front of these horrible, vile men.

Sending a prayer up for her grandpa's spirit to swiftly pass painlessly to the spirit side, she saw her mother with her arms clutching a bundle, tears silently falling down her face. The proud, unshakeable confidence Agasga normally possessed was gone.

Where were her best friend and his heavily pregnant wife and children? She did not see them. She hoped they had not come or had gotten away. Her friend usually stayed away from the group when he felt trouble was near. He had instincts and signs from the spirits and ancestors, so he could have gone a different way if he had been told to. Maybe.

After a few hours of walking, the crying and wailing had stopped.

~~~

Four days into their northern march, the weather had shifted. It was much colder up here and many of her remaining people did not have blankets to keep them warm. Their food supplies were almost empty as well, since much of it had been left on the ground with their dead.

If they tried to talk amongst themselves, the troops would come and beat them. None of them knew how much longer they would march nor how they could catch food if they weren't allowed any weapons or help.

She could feel the desperation from a few of her tribe. Two were mothers who had watched their children die. They had nothing left to lose and there was no way for her to tell them to wait and watch.

When they stopped each night, the troops would build the tribe one single fire to sleep around but one fire did nothing for fifty people! The ones without blankets were hand gestured to sleep around the fire and huddle with each other.

Each night, Sitting Bear would go around seeing if any others had been lost due to the cold temperatures or the lengthy march killing them. She would guide children to mothers in a hope that nobody else would die and each mother would take care of the poor child she had placed next to them.

All of the women would nod their heads in agreement once she ushered the child towards them, and she would silently pray for the woman to give the child food and love for as long as possible.

The troops did not share their food with any of the tribe. Of course not, she thought; they did not care if all of her people starved on the way to the government land.

She had placed two children in the care of Agasga on the first night. Her mother seemed content to take care of them, knowing that Sitting Bear would look after her brother.

~~~

On the sixth day, it started snowing.

She could not tell how long they had marched, as the days were all blurring together.

The landscape was becoming more barren and the trees were sparse.

A few of the younger children had been too weak to walk this morning. All of the women took turns carrying them but they knew deep in their hearts that without food and blankets, the children would die.

The food was completely gone at this point. They grabbed leaves and grass to eat along the way, not knowing what else to do.

The troops knew that they had run out of food. One of the guards had approached the leader with this news and the leader simply shrugged and looked away.

There was nothing to do but continue living and walking.

~~~

She woke up and found her mother dead on the eighth day. The little girl that Agasga had looked after told her that Agasga had been giving everything she had to eat to the girl and her brother.

There was no time to bury her mother as they were forced to march away from the camp. Sitting Bear didn't even have time to take in Agasga's final acts of compassion.

Others had died, but seeing her mother's frozen face had given her a feeling of apprehension, despair and dread. If any of them made it out of this alive, it would only be due to the protection of their ancestors.

The men marching them north were unfeeling and inhuman.

If she had any energy, she would feel anger towards them; yet she knew that she had to keep her strength to keep walking. She must stay alive for her brother.

As she glanced at Adohi, she noticed that he was shivering from the coldness. She covered him with her blanket and continued to rub her arms.

Their silence was broken only by the sounds of the horses, walking in the snow with a crunching noise that urged the tribe forward.

~~~

They finished their walk at the end of the tenth day. Four children had fallen and not gotten up that day.

She could not carry a child anymore, nor could any of the other women.

It was so cold. A freezing chill had settled into her bones and her body ached.

The troops ushered them towards a hill area that was slightly sheltered against the wind. Oh, how the wind howled and moaned.

Looking around, she could not see any trees or anything to use as firewood.

Scraping her foot against the ground, she saw that under the top layer of snow was hard brown dirt.

How would they survive? This was only the beginning of winter. What would happen once winter blew in its hard snows and even colder temperatures?

Surely, the men would not leave them with nothing, she thought. Could their white government really be this cruel?

~~~

The next morning she awoke with a start. She heard and saw the troops packing, getting ready to leave.

Her people could walk no further.

She approached the leader who sat on top of his horse, watching his men pack the rest of their belongings. "We can walk no further. We are starving and have no way to hunt or gather food."

The leader looked at her with anger burning out of his eyes. "That is not my problem. My orders were to get you here and that is what I have done."

"How can you just leave us here? We have no food, no blankets. The children are starving and freezing to death!"

He stared at her with disgust mixed with hatred. Why so much hatred, she thought? We have done nothing to him.

"Please give us something. Give us food or a few spare blankets. We will die if you leave us like this!"

"I do not owe you anything," he said with a snarl. "You get to fend for yourself. Now get back in line with your people!"

"How can you do this? What kind of man are you?"

"What kind of man am I? I am a man who runs this land; that is what kind of man. And you are nothing. Worse than nothing. You are dirt and you will die in the dirt you stand upon now."

She could not help but start to cry; exhaustion and fear reaching their breaking-point equally in her body. Rubbing her arms to comfort herself and try to spread some warmth, she said loudly enough for most of the camp to hear, "You are the worst kind of man. You have killed so many women and children, your spirit must be dead! You bring no honor to yourself and your people because your spirit is dead."

Tears streaming down her face, she turned and walked back to join her brother.

Sitting Bear heard the gunshot before she felt anything. Adohi's eyes became huge as he stared at her chest and ran towards her.

Looking down at her left breast, she saw bright red blood spreading along her dirty and stained dress. As she dropped to the snowy ground, all she felt was the cold. It was so cold. The cold was everywhere. She could not feel her feet or hands anymore.

Her breathing became shallow as her lungs were unable to draw in a complete breath. She could not breathe. A panic rose up in her body as the coldness continued to spread. Her hands flew up to her chest as she continued to fight for a deep breath.

Her brother held her hand with tears streaming down his face silently willing her not to die. She tried to smile at Adohi but could only blink.

What a horrible, cold way to die, she thought, as her last full-body shivers were replaced with the serenity of death.

A few lessons learned in this lifetime:

A strict upbringing coupled with no push back or fighting for what you truly want out of life, for example standing up to her mother by being her lesbian (two-spirited) self or studying under the medicine man, leads to an unfulfilled and pointless life. She did not stand up for her soul journey in this lifetime and died tragically while still young.

Chapter 6

The Viking King

956 CE

The world was getting smaller and Vikings were raiding everywhere from Ireland to France, Morocco to Russia, settling in places from Iceland to North Africa, and 'discovering' America and Canada 400 years before Columbus. The ferocity of the Viking culture was as strong as their worship of the gods, and kings were only as tough and long-lived as their minds and bodies allowed. Their homelands were heavily sought after by other aspiring Viking kings and Sweden, at this time, was no exception.

The fire alarm was raised in the middle of the night. Jumping up quickly, I threw on my clothes and ran out the door. All of our buildings were made of wood and if one caught fire, we would need all of the townspeople to throw water on the surrounding buildings in order to stop the spread.

My wife, Nuba, said from the bed, "Should I come with you?"

I glanced back at her as I walked towards the door and replied, "No, my love, stay with the children. It is the fire alarm and we should have the fire put out in a few hours at most." I smiled at her and then ran out.

My guards came with me and we rushed towards the fire raging at the edge of the town. It was next to the blacksmith's hut and had only claimed two houses at this point. My people in the surrounding homes were already forming the water lines, moving the water buckets between the well and the buildings closest to the fire.

As I shouted orders to everyone to soak the huts around the fire, I ran to gather more buckets from my own house. Rounding the corner of a hut closest to my home, I heard a movement and then everything went black as I fell to the ground.

~~~

I woke up with a groan.

My head pounding mercilessly as if it had just been trampled on by a dozen horses. Someone had hit me with something and knocked me out completely.

My hands were tied behind my back. My mouth was full of a cloth tied around my head.

Furious, I glanced around the room I was alone in. There was no light coming in which meant it was still in the middle of the night or that I was being kept in a dark hole somewhere. But I could feel the wooden panels of a hut with my hands, so I knew that I was in someone's house.

I tried to yell, yet the sound was stifled due to the cloth.

Where were my guards? Where was my wife, my children? Who had done this?

It could be anybody, really.

I was not simply a commoner.

I am the dreaded invader, King Harald. I have many slaves, many riches, and many children. I have a beautiful wife and a life that all men envy.

There was nothing that I could not do nor anywhere I could not go. I had seen more lands in my thirty years than most could even dream of in one hundred years.

My life was written by the gods. My mother had told me of her vision after she had visited the sacred stones of our people on the mountain.

She was a beautiful, fierce warrior. Her strength had been legendary. She had birthed me two nights before a battle and had led her men to an undeniable victory to gain more land from a neighboring king the following evening. Her attack at night had not only led to the complete annihilation of the opponent's forces, it was legendary in that every single man fighting for that king had died, in the dead of night, under a full moon, by a woman who had just given birth and was fighting for her right to sit on the throne until her newborn son could claim it.

She achieved that and so much more.

My father, Fenrir, had been killed valiantly when a visiting king from the east had come to claim lands that were not his. Once Fenrir, had challenged the foreign king as he sat at Fenrir's table telling long tales about owning our land, there was no going back.

The wounds my father sustained from that fight had eventually killed him one week and two days later. However, the visiting king had died on that fateful day. This day also happened to be when our neighboring king, Erik, had decided to start stealing livestock and women.

The day that my mother, Eda, had prayed from before sunrise at the stones for my father's life, here, she had the vision of my life. She had felt a warmth rise out of the ground and wrap around her belly, supporting her while a humming rose out of the earth that grew louder.

All of the clouds left the sky and the sun shone brightly on this spot, lighting up my mother. There were no other sounds; no birds squawking, no trees rustling, and the air held a pregnant pause.

Eda's vision showed my bloody birth that would dictate my future; I came into a battle and I would leave in a battle.

I would be a mighty king and rule long and well. My reign for my people would bring wealth and land, years without war and much expansion for trade.

There was nothing that I would not be able to achieve because that is what was seen and foretold.

That knowing deep down in my own soul, created my unstoppable momentum and fearlessness. I knew who I was and what would happen. It was my destiny and I embraced it wholeheartedly and entirely.

~~~

When I was 15, I had gone to the top of a sacred mountain to see a renowned seer, one that could tell me what my future would hold and when I would die. I did not fully understand my mother's vision and I wanted it confirmed.

I had grown up without a father, who would have told me to never doubt my mother's visions because Eda was always right. She had seen another vision come to pass, that Fenrir would die a week after the fight. Her only course of action was to tell him so that he could right anything that needed taken care of before he died.

Fenrir had sent word to his younger brother to come and help my mother hold the throne for me. My uncle was a farmer and he loved the land. He hated the big gathering hall and the town that had sprung up around it; he wanted the fresh air and he loved talking to his animals. His wife was a simple farm wife and kept busy with their three children. My uncle also supported his wife's parents and brother with his massive farm. The animals he bred were the best in the land and he was even getting offers from other kingdoms to supply them with animals that could breed.

Yet my uncle, Gustaf, heeded my father's call, for Fenrir had always given him anything he needed in order to make his lands flourish and children grow. Their bond as children had made them close even though their paths were completely different. There had never been the usual sibling jealousy or betrayal, only love, support, and a bit of fighting as all young boys do. Then there was some distance when Fenrir went off to pursue his dreams and become king. After years of voyaging, pillaging he returned to our homeland with many large chests of gold to claim his throne.

My mother had been one of the previous king's daughters. As soon as my father saw her in the hall, Fenrir knew she would be his wife. Fenrir proceeded to give her gifts and charm her until she said yes to becoming his wife.

Their love was different and long lasting in this culture of free flowing, partner exchange.

Thus, both the brothers had true love with their wives, and that was passed to their children. I believed in true love but when I was fifteen, I was lost.

My uncle had only stayed for the first three years of my life, visiting his wife and family on his farm once per year. After a lengthy discussion with my mother about the length of time he had been away from his own family while wanting to fulfill his oath to my father, Gustaf returned home. She did not want to make him stay away from his wife and his dreams, and Gustaf thought Eda was strong enough to hold the throne until I was older.

The people loved Eda, as they had my father and her father.

In my childhood, I did not understand why my uncle went away. After he left when I was three, Gustaf visited yearly and would stay for three weeks only. During these visits he showed me what it was to be a man; he also told me stories of my father and gave me the warm love of an uncle.

I always hoped he would stay longer or move closer with his family but it was not his fate. Gustaf kept up his annual visits until I went off viking at the manly age of seventeen.

Apparently, Gustaf and my father looked very similar. As I grew older, I could see on my mother's face that it sometimes pained her to look upon my uncle.

The certainty of my mother, regarding her vision of my destiny, rubbed off on me and I had accepted it until I turned fifteen. Something about that birthday caused me to seek another opinion, which led me to the old seer on the sacred mountain.

~~~

Into her dark cave I went, and sitting down by the fire, she smeared my face with the blood of a rabbit and chanted around me. Her eyes rolled back in her head and I felt the change in the air around me.

Another being was present in that cave, and the seer began to speak in a strange voice with her head thrown back facing up to the sky.

She told me of the battles I would wage and win, the gold I would accumulate that would rival the most mythical kings of old, the women I would have, and the sons my wife would bear. I would have only one daughter and she would be a treasure to me as well.

Then she abruptly stopped with a small gurgle coming out of her upturned mouth. Her eyes rolled back to their normal position and she stared at me.

"Is that all?" I inquired.

She confusingly nodded no as she said, "Yes." Then she cackled. "There is more but I will not tell you for it might shape your actions and you must live your destiny on your own terms, young Harald. It is needed at this time."

"You will not tell me?" I asked her.

"I will tell you when you are older. Come to me when you are twenty-five and I will tell you all."

"Ten years from now? What kind of seer are you?"

"The old and wise kind. A true seer does not shape the future of the person before her, but it is possible to change events that occur with her words. If one part of your destiny could be affected by what I tell you, then I cannot. That is what your ancestors are saying about the second portion of your life. They are your guides and I can see them."

Frustrated at not being told all, I replied, "Who are my guides? Why can't I see them?"

"You know them, Harald. They talk to you in the wind and they are the reason you take certain actions. They are all around you. One is your grandfather, the king. Another is your father's mother."

"Strange," I responded.

"Call on them for guidance when you need help or clarity. I will not be around forever to guide you nor will you stay here very long. You leave for your first voyage in two years."

This was not a surprise to me. I was ready to leave now but knew I had to build my strength up so that I could not be defeated by the man who trained me. Once I had bested him, then I could have proper battles with new enemies far and wide.

If a man cannot best his opponent, he had no right to lead men into battle or even become a king.

"Your mother will rule while you prove you are worthy to be a Viking king. After three years of this, there will be much recognition, wealth and slaves that you return home with. Five years hence, you will come see me and I will tell you all. Perhaps by then, through your own actions, you will have a different destiny that I will see. Perhaps yes. Perhaps no. Perhaps you won't be able to find the time as King Harald," she chucked, the whites of her eyes visible for a split-second, with her mouth caught in a wide grin, before she saw his eyes, and immediately composed herself, looking down somberly.

Knowing I would get nothing more from her, I said, "I will see you in ten years, Seer. Thank you for your service."

"Hold true to your destiny, young Harald. You are a great king."

Leaving her with a gold cup and silver coin in payment for her words, I knew that Eda's vision had been the truth. That would be the last time I sought another's word over my mother's.

~~~

Lying on the dirt floor, unable to raise myself from where I had been thrown, I wondered why I had not returned to see that old seer.

Why had I not taken the time out of my kingly duties? Would she have warned me of this very situation?

There was no use thinking about it now, I realized. What was done was done.

I heard no sounds coming from outside the hut, not even the sound of a warrior guarding me. If I could find something to get the ropes off of my hands or at least the cloth out of my mouth, I could free myself.

Then I would find out who was behind this and where my wife and children were.

Searching every inch of the hut, there was only a large stone used to sharpen knives. I could rub the ropes around my wrists on the corner of that stone until they were worn through.

I shimmied towards the stone like a snake slithering on the ground. Using the stone to slowly inch myself up until I was sitting upright, I started rubbing the ropes that bound my wrists against the stone.

The ropes were not small. 'This was going to take a while,' I thought as I continued the movement that would free my hands.

I kept my ears open for any sounds outside the hut as my mind wandered into the past.

~~~

When I returned to my home at age twenty, my mother greeted me and showed me her improvements she had made in my absence. The town itself was heavily guarded and secured with a giant wooden wall the same height as trees. The people looked happy and the kingdom was prosperous.

"So much has changed while I've been away," I said without any regrets.

"Yes, it has, my son. I also have a few women for you that would make suitable wives. You don't need to marry one now, but it would help secure your throne if you could start having children soon."

"I have had many women, mother. But I will look at your women and if one suits, I will agree. It is time to take a bride before I leave on this next trip. You will look after her while I'm away."

"How long do you wish to be away?"

"One more year, at least."

"Then it is so. You *are* the great king. I saw you becoming so many moons ago."

"Not yet, mother. Soon. I will be that king and more."

"Now come, your youngest cousins are here. They wish to go viking with you," she said.

"How many children did uncle have again? I lost count years ago."

She laughed. "Gustaf had three before he came here to help me when your father died. Then a new baby every time he visited his wife for the next three years. Then two more after and all of them lived to adulthood. So, eight children in total. Five love the farming life and have settled with families on your uncle's land. Three of them are here to go with you."

"Three? Uncle must be furious!", I exclaimed.

"No," she said, "he came with them when they arrived two weeks ago. Gustaf gave his blessing and stayed for a few days to discuss new ideas with me. He left last week. I think you should go and see him before you leave again. He does miss you."

We had made it back to our home, the grand hall. It was even more beautiful and large with my mother's improvements.

"Is it still strange for you to see uncle after all of these years? As much as he looks like my father?" I questioned her.

"No, not anymore, Harald. It used to pain me because Fenrir's loss was so recent. Now it makes me happy. Gustaf is like my brother after all of this time. And you, my son, are the spitting image of your father at the same age. I see so much of him in you, as well as many of my traits. You are wise and kind, a warrior and a lover."

"Ha! A lover! Now that will be the day mother. But I have missed you." I joked. Giving her a big hug and kiss, I laughingly left the hall to pursue the warm bed of the beautiful girl I had seen in by the blacksmith's hut. She would be a nice welcome home present.

~~~

My mother's choice in women was quite charming. She had chosen one of every colored hair – red, blonde, brown and black – because she had no idea what my preference would be. Two were from neighboring kingdoms whose kings had requested an alliance with me based on marriage to their daughters.

As she paraded them before me, I noticed that only one of them caught my attention. There was something about the redhead that I couldn't explain. Her green eyes were strange and slightly tilted, as if she was from the Far East. We had run into men from the Far East selling beautiful silks and foreign herbs and every one of them had similar tilting eyes.

Her body was slender and she was very short. This appealed to me compared to the normal women in my kingdom that were similar to my mother; tall, curvaceous, and blonde.

I nodded at my mother, and Eda came close enough to whisper, "Has one caught your eye, my son?"

"Yes. The redhead. Tell me more about her."

"Ladies, please leave us. Thank you for your time," mother said to them in a loud voice.

Then she turned and looked at me.

"I knew you would find her intriguing. She is the daughter of the king to our east. He married a princess from the Far East, and Nuba is their oldest daughter."

"That would explain the eyes. Has she any other qualities?"

"She is well versed in old stories and myths. I have watched Nuba and she has different customs based on the moon and stars. She stays to herself and is very happy with her own company. She also speaks three languages."

"That is ideal. Can you bring Nuba to me so that I might speak with her in a more relaxed setting? Perhaps in our small dining area and not the large hall," I asked.

"Of course. You should know that she is not here of her own accord. Her father has sent her as an alliance and trade expansion. However, from what Nuba has said, she has no other lover nor has ever had that chance. She was closely guarded and allowed only access to her mother in privacy. All of her moves were watched and she has never experienced such freedom as I have allowed her here. She is very grateful for the time she has to spend freely in our kingdom."

That was curious. Her father had kept her under lock and key. Why?

Bowing my head towards my mother, I went to my chamber to freshen up and relax. The servants came in and placed large bowls of fruit and bread on my table, as well as wine and water.

My wife would need to be as thoughtful and overseeing as Eda was.

After a while of eating and drinking at my table, the redhead was introduced to me by my mother.

"Thank you, mother," I smiled, as Eda tilted her head slightly towards me before promptly leaving the room.

I turned to this enchanting woman, who, upon closer study of her face, could not have been more than seventeen years old. She wore a bracelet of jade which I knew was some sort of protection given to her by her mother from the East.

"Tell me about yourself, Nuba. What do you want out of life?" I asked.

Her right eyebrow rose up. "That is a strange question coming from a king," she said. "Shouldn't you demand that I take my clothes off so you can see how shapely my body is for bearing you sons?" she joked.

I threw my head back and laughed. She was spirited, just my kind of woman.

"Please, sit down." I beckoned to the other seat at the table. "Let us relax and get to know each other. I already know how beautiful and exotic you are. Now, I want to know what you desire. I will tell you what I desire, and we will see if we can meet in the middle to make a good marriage." I said with a playful smile.

"I appreciate your directness, my king." Gingerly, Nuba sat down on the seat next to mine at the table. Taking a bit of the bread, she shyly put a small piece in her mouth.

Looking at me directly in the eyes, she started expressing her dreams. "I wish to grow the herbs and plants that I love for my food. I want to learn how to make jewelry and throw knives, things I was never allowed to do in my father's home. I want to pick my own dresses and do my own hair. My husband must be fair and a king, for that is my worth as a king's daughter. But I want love from my husband and to feel peace when he is around. I never felt peace around my father or his bodyguards. It is very stifling. I enjoy the freedom that I have here – freedom to walk in the forest or up a hill, to speak with whomever I choose. To take my time and learn new customs. It is all fun and pleasant."

"And do you long for children?"

"I know that children will come and I welcome that time. But I wish to enjoy my freedom for a little bit longer here," she smiled at me then, and it almost took my breath away.

Her entire face lit up when she smiled, and I could only stare in an enchanted gaze. Beholding her in this happy thought was to come face to face with a goddess. It was as if there was light coming off of her skin and making the area around her dance with her happiness.

How could I deny Nuba that freedom when I wanted the same? Although it was different for men than women regarding children and raise them; some women did choose to come viking and that was normal. Yet this woman was expected to be a queen from her birth and had been raised to a certain standard.

Even though my mother had been a warrior and led her men into battle, this woman would not. I did not want a woman similar to Eda in that way. I wanted the exotic mystery that this woman effortlessly displayed.

I smiled back at her. "I too wish to remain childless for a little while longer. I will be going away for a short while again in order to bolster my riches and supplies, to gain more slaves and land, and to bring back new items, and culture from far off places. Then I will come back to settle down. To be the king my mother has raised and my father will be proud of from Valhalla. Will you get to know me a bit before I leave? I would like the opportunity to know you better, Nuba."

She nodded her head and said, "I would enjoy that. I will see you soon." Standing from the table, she left the room with a backwards glance and smile.

I grinned and continued eating. I couldn't wait for our next conversation.

~~~

Nuba and I spent many days together in the coming two weeks before I left. As we got to know more of each other, we seemed to fit together very well.

The night before I was to leave, I asked her if she would be my wife upon my return.

"I will wait for you, my king. Do not forget me while you are away," she answered.

I smiled at her and replied, "I could never forget you, Nuba. You are a goddess."

"My name means goddess of drought when there has been too much rain. It is from my mother's people," she said.

"Nuba, goddess of drought, I cannot wait until we are married. You have enchanted me."

Without warning, she picked up my left hand and pressed her lips to the back of it. She smiled timidly at me and then left the room without looking back.

My heart was beating rapidly and my hands felt very sweaty. I wiped them on my shirt and shook my head to clear the fog brought on by her kissing my hand.

Was this love?

~~~

I heard footsteps outside the hut. I tested the ropes. They were not weak enough yet.

'Odin, where are you?!' I beseeched the mighty god in my head.

Daylight was coming in through the cracks in the wood of the hut.

A mountain of a man opened the door and came inside. Grabbing me by the elbow, he hoisted me up easily as if I were a small bag of grain. Pushing me forward through the doorway, I noticed that two more men were outside, nodding and smiling at me.

I had never seen any of them before.

As the man paraded me through my own town, my own kingdom, towards the very middle of the village, I heard women crying and children whispering but I could see nobody.

We approached a circle of armed men in the market clearing and I saw that many of them were hired from outside of my kingdom; they wore bright colors compared to our blues and browns, and cut their hair differently.

The massive man grasped my elbow even tighter and forced me down upon my knees.

A wailing cry went up from the women. I could not see where they were but they must be close if they could see me.

Sooner or later, the man responsible for all of this would show himself.

I had a feeling that I knew exactly who was behind this.

Why had I ever allowed that poisonous woman into my kingdom? For trade and glory and gold?

~~~

I shook my head in disbelief.

I really could not fathom why I had agreed that this offensive woman would marry my cousin, Kol. Regardless of the fact that she was a king's daughter (illegitimate, most likely) and she was the reason our trade route expanded into Gaul (Frankia) – she was the biggest pain I had ever come across in another human being.

She demanded to be kept in my boat and tried to flirt with me every day despite knowing I was to be married upon arrival home. Day after day, Amira kept at it, begging me to take her as my wife to which I firmly refused. However, she also flirted with everyone else. I suspected that she had slept with some of the men but could not be certain.

Kol was completely bewitched by her and could not see past her beauty, the same with most of my men on the other boats. I felt that at any moment, Amira might tell the strongest of my warriors that she would marry the first one that overthrew me, my men and my cousins.

She was not to be trusted, and this I felt deeply. How could my cousin not see this?

I spoke to my closest guard and friend about throwing her overboard and if we could make it look like an accident. The only way that it could be done is if a huge storm came and rain fell. Then we would have the chance to be done with her, throw her to the sea gods and nobody would see it due to the rain.

Praying to Odin and Thor, I knew there were only so many days before we reached home.

If there was no storm, other plans would have to be made.

The trading terms that I had reached with her father would benefit both kingdoms for generations to come. Money would flow in without me having to raid more settlements and cities. Her father would never know she died at sea for many years, if ever. She was not worth the trouble she would bring.

Her father had simply wanted her out of his house. She was a nightmare dressed as a beautiful woman.

I was unsure of how getting her back to my home would go because I knew deep in my bones that she most certainly would cause trouble. It was her nature.

I would ask Kol to take her to his parent's farm immediately after their wedding. Or before.

Anything to get her out of my way for a few months. I wanted to enjoy my beautiful red-headed bride without worrying about this insufferable woman that tried to play men upon each other.

~~~

My marriage was a sacred event that my bride and I enjoyed entirely.

Everyone from the town and the outskirts came to our wedding, along with kings from neighboring kingdoms that I had alliances with.

My mother had arranged everything perfectly. Nuba looked stunning, with a long green dress and purple flowers in her hair, and we were united under the trees at the entrance of the forest. The old seer attended the event and blessed our marriage.

Lightening splintered the sky, a sign that Thor approved of our union.

I wore my crown, the same crown my father had worn and my mother's father before him, and a newly blackened leather ensemble made especially for this magnificent day.

Everyone cheered as we kissed and we led everyone back into the great hall, where our family rooms were at the back of.

The great hall held a feast that had been prepared and laid out for our enjoyment; many pigs, geese, sheep and cows were cooked. Everyone ate and drank to their heart's content. Games were played and people grew boisterous.

The hall was cheerful and bright.

I looked at Nuba and leaned down to whisper into her ear, "Shall we head to our room now? I wish to be alone with you."

She smiled up at me and nodded.

Grabbing her hand, we made our way to our bedroom at the back of the hall. The fire was roaring and plates of extra food had been laid on the table. Wine and fruit was there as well.

I closed the door and walked to my wife, my Nuba, my goddess.

Taking her in my arms, I realized that I never wanted to let her go. She was even more beautiful than I remembered before I had left on my raids.

"How I have missed you! Have you missed me?" I asked her.

She looked up at me with eyes full of love and wonder. "Yes, my Viking king. I have missed you and thought of you every day. Did you think of me?"

"I did."

Smiling softly, she kissed me. I lifted her into my arms and carried her to our bed.

~~~

As my queen and I spent more time together, she became pregnant and I made our kingdom more impenetrable while I sent warriors on missions to increase our fortunes and trade routes. I wanted our kingdom to surpass all other kingdoms; to embrace inevitable change and growth, to allow new cultures in without forgetting our own.

All peoples were allowed except for the Christians.

They were all insane and had a backwards view on living and dying. They thought a person lived more after they died, and if they suffered more on earth, the better it would be for them in death; as if suffering helped a person in the afterlife!

Christians chose not to enjoy this life and to make themselves miserable instead, as well as everyone around them. Meanwhile, their priests grew as fat as their chests of gold while they yelled at the common folk to stay poor and give all of their money, food and lives to a dead god on a cross.

Thus, they were not allowed in my hall or in my kingdom.

It was hard enough to trade with kings that fell under the Christian way of life or their dress wearing ruler, the pope. I had heard what the pope demanded of the kings that followed him, the fortune he amassed in the name of 'keeping the peace' and expanding the Christian religion.

The only person that had thought to challenge my refusal to let Christians into my kingdom was Amira, my cousin's wife now. She had asked me at a family dinner how it was possible that I allowed all others in besides Christians.

It was widely known that Christians had much wealth, especially the priests and the landholders for the Church.

"Why aren't you attacking these unguarded landholders or priests after you gain the information that you need from visiting Christians?" she questioned me.

Glancing around the dinner table, I saw that most of my family agreed with what she had said.

"I do not want to involve myself in anything with Christians, besides the few Christian kings that I have trade alliances with, including your father. I especially do not want to draw notice to my kingdom from the pope and his substantial army," I responded.

Christians represented a plague to me; one that was trying to wipe out freedom and the joy of living along with meeting my father in Valhalla.

"Yes, but why not take their money under the guise of another kingdom so that it is not traced back here to your kingdom?" Amira asked.

"If the pope were to call all of his Christian kings and landholders to take up the banner to stop the taking of his gold, it would be the end to Vikings across the world, not just this kingdom," I stated.

The pope would stop at nothing to expand his kingdom and riches.

"How much harm could be done if you strategically attacked two or three of the landholders or priests in different areas? The least guarded ones? Nobody would know it was you if you burned the entire village," she replied.

"I am not guided by the gods to do this. If they said to do this raiding and burning, then I would do it. For now, I have been told not to let the Christians in, ever, and that is enough."

"Surely you are not scared of them? I lived amongst them and came from a Christian king. They do sit on massive amounts of gold. All of the kings and landholders do. You are missing out on the biggest wealth that you could easily gain," Amira quipped, thinking her goading would get me to agree with her schemes.

I slammed my hand down on the table. "Enough. I am the king here and this is my decision."

Everyone was looking down at their laps, afraid to look me in the eye, all except Amira, who was staring at me with a smirk on her face.

I would not take back talk, divisive scheming or whatever she thought she was doing. The last person I would ever take raiding or war advice from was Amira.

Apparently, she felt differently.

~~~

One year after this family dinner, while my wife was in childbirth with our second child, I found out that fifty of my cousin's men had attacked a Christian landowner near to Amira's home port town.

They had slaughtered almost everyone in the village and fortress and took a mountain of gold from the landowner's home. The only people that the Vikings allowed to live were five warriors that joined forces with them and ten young women that were taken for slaves.

The only reason I found out was that one of the women that attended my wife was a young woman I had never seen before. She was a healer from this Christian landowner's village. There was no love lost as she related the story because she had been an outcast from the village as a pagan for practicing healing arts.

My rage boiled up. I bellowed for my mother who came running from my wife's bedside. As I told Eda the story, she looked worried.

"This is not good, my son. We have lived in peace for so many years now. This could undo everything you and I have worked for, especially all of the trade routes. What are the chances that the raiding party was not seen at all? That nobody could identify them as Viking?"

"That is the dilemma. Not to mention that now we have a problem with trust and loyalty in my kingdom. How to punish Kol after he expressly disobeyed my orders. He was my heir, but with the birth last year of my son, he is no longer needed as that." I answered.

"Let us discuss this after your child has arrived, Harald," my mother said. "For now, there is nothing to be done and this must be thought upon long and hard. Your actions here will have long-term consequences."

"Yes, they will. Every decision I make has long term consequences. Hurry back to my wife, mother."

I stared at the wall as she left the room.

What should I do to my cousin? The last thing I needed was a blood feud with my own cousins after so many years of peace throughout my land.

~~~

As the excitement of my new child and an attack from a neighboring kingdom against my uncle's ever growing farm took my precious time in the coming months, this episode of betrayal by my cousin was pushed to the side.

Despite my distraction, I had Kol watched by one of my most trusted men. There seemed to be a halt to the raiding and no new treachery was taking place.

Two years after the birth of my second child, another son, I decreed that they were now my heirs in a public ceremony which was blessed by our town's elders.

I should have paid closer attention to who did or did not attend this ceremony, and the faces of those who did. A king should always be watchful.

Having long forgotten my promise to pay a visit to the reclusive seer that I had sought out ten years ago, my twenty-fifth year on this rocky land passed with the birth of a daughter. My wife and I were happy that the gods had blessed us with children that were strong and healthy.

Nuba taught them many of her ways that had been passed down by her mother, and I showed them the Viking ways, of the land where they lived.

Our family was close and loving with my mother's guidance and ease out of public life giving her the opportunity to be a doting grandmother.

~ ~ ~

Looking back on all of this now, I see that there were so many signs that I missed and opportunities to help me shape a different future. At the age of thirty, there had been plenty of time for reflection notwithstanding being a king.

The huge mountainous man picked me up from my numbed knees to stand as the crowd around me grew larger.

I stared down at my feet thinking about kicking him in his privates with my hands tied behind my back. I would not be able to get very far, even if I momentarily hurt him.

He yanked the cloth in my mouth down so that I was able to speak.

"Who are you? Who do you serve," I questioned him hoarsely. My throat was dry from the cloth and trying to breathe around it.

He did not even look at me and I could see more and more of my people, subdued by more men, walking to the circle and staring at me.

I could feel their energy and their eyes, willing me to do something, to have some plan to get out of this hostage situation.

Yet I had nothing.

I glanced around the circle and knew. All of my best men, all of my warriors, all of them were dead.

The only people looking back at me were women, children and men that did not fight.

Where was my wife? My children?

~~~

The crowd opened and Kol came marching through it with a wicked grin on his face.

"On your knees!" my cousin shouted at me.

I glared back at him with my head high, refusing his demand.

My stomach sank because I knew what would happen now. All of my regrets came rushing to me; how I should have had Amira killed on the boat or shortly after; how I should have gone to see the seer; how I should have known as a king to never to trust anyone, even a cousin!

How had Kol forgotten that we were family? That our fathers shared an unbreakable bond and that is the reason why I considered him a brother? That I had shared everything with him? He would still be stuck on that farm if I had refused to take him viking with me all those years ago.

"This is not you, cousin. This is Amira's way, not ours. Why have you forgotten everything Gustaf taught you? You were like a brother to me. I gave you everything and shared my spoils with you! I let Amira come here and marry you."

"I don't need your brotherhood or your permission, Harald. I have your kingdom now," Kol proclaimed as he kicked my knees.

Falling to the ground, I tried to sit upright but could not without the help of my arms that were still secured behind my back.

"Haven't you ever wondered why Amira never gave you a child? Why she is always scheming for more? Why she pushed you to take my kingdom?" I yelled at him.

"Silence! I do not wish to hear your lies," Kol snapped back at me. "We have gone too far now. And you needn't worry about my wife. Because Amira has not given me any children, I will be taking another wife that I know will provide children. I will take your wife and your children, along with everything you once owned. It is all mine now."

The rage that welled up with me warred with the bile that was climbing up the back of my throat. I refused to allow him to see my rage, but my body's response was natural; my cousin even touching Nuba or my children made me curse him in my head.

He laughed cruelly.

"Everything that you worked so hard for, the peace you wanted to keep for so long, the loving family you wanted to raise. All of it, wiped out in a matter of one night. How does that feel, cousin?"

Jeering at me, he looked up into the crowd as it parted again.

From behind me came his wife, Amira. The horrible creature that was behind all of this and all of the attacks on Christian landowners we had heard coming in for years now.

She was gloating because she knew she had won.

"You always were so hard-headed, Harald," she remarked. "But look at you now, the mighty king Harald, felled by his own cousin. What a sad day for you."

Amira started laughing until she was doubled over with tears coming out of her eyes.

I refused to look at her.

Grabbing my chin with her hand, she hissed, "You could have made me your queen. Instead, I have made myself the queen!"

I snatched my head back from her grasp.

"You will never be a true queen. You cannot have children because you were with so many men at a young age. You are a dried up barren woman," I laughed up at her. "Kol, did she tell you how many men she was with before you, before she came to live in our homeland? Amira has used you all of these years for money and power. Nothing else. She does not love you and never has. If I had given her a chance, she would have settled for being my mistress, as long as she could have had money and power."

Amira pulled her hand back and slapped me across the face.

My cousin looked shocked before his face hardened into a stony mask; I had hit a nerve. I started to laugh hysterically.

"It matters not. Amira has served me well and motivated me to take what's mine. She does not mind that I will take Nuba as my second wife," Kol retorted with a smile.

It was Amira's turn to look startled. Evidently, this was not part of her plan.

"Oh, Amira. It seems you do not like this idea." I said contemptuously. "It is alright, you will be replaced since your womb is unfertile and your dark ways will lessen as your power shrinks. My cousin will stop listening to you and eventually, you will be killed, just as I am about to be."

It was my turn to smile and feel some joy at the thought of her subsequent death. I knew in my heart someone would murder her even if it wasn't Kol.

Glowering at me, Amira walked to Kol's side.

"Just do it. Do it now! He has lived long enough," she exclaimed.

Shouting so that all around could hear me, I proclaimed, "Yes, cousin, let the Christian woman tell you what to do. I am sure she does command you in all matters. How do your men feel being led by a Christian woman who's proxy is you?"

Rage flickered in my cousin's eyes. Glancing around at his men, who had shifted uncomfortably in their boots, Kol looked back at me with anger etched on his face.

"It is I who have taken your kingdom, your wife, your children, your gold, your ships, and everything else you hold dear. My name will be spoken of long after you are dust. Say goodbye to your wife now."

Gesturing his head to the left, I looked over and saw that my cousin's men had brought my wife into the circle. Tears were streaming down her face.

"I love you, Harald," Nuba said to me, her voice trembling. She was not a Viking warrior woman; she was more feminine, soft, and did not belong in this fight.

It was my fault that she was here; my oversight, my arrogance, my greed.

"I love you, my love. Never forget how much," I told her.

"They killed your mother," she cried harder.

"Then I join her in Valhalla," I bravely told my wife and bowed my head to Nuba in acceptance.

Wheeling my head around, I gazed at my cousin. "I cannot believe that you killed my mother!" I screamed at him. "Smart to kill the woman that would have murdered you in your sleep and taken the kingdom back for my sons. I curse you and your bloodline. None of your sons or daughters will live longer than thirty days so that you will know the pain of loss. I will be back to kill you and take what is mine."

Lightning struck at that moment. I laughed up at the lightning and declared, "Odin has affirmed it! You will lose every…"

That was all I had time to say before my head flew from my body towards the ground.

As I floated above my body and headed into the clouds, I could see the stunned faces of the village women, the mountain of a man with his axe soaked in my blood, and Nuba crying uncontrollably next to my headless body.

I knew; I would be back.

A few lessons learned in this lifetime:

If you follow your intuition instead of letting life happen to you, you will go far. Listen to your elders, and learn from wise/energetically powerful people instead of thinking you know everything. Unchecked greed leads to your downfall, and letting your social network influence your decisions to allow people into your energy (your kingdom) is reckless.

Chapter 7

The Hunted Wife

❖

1398 CE

The region known today as Romania was under partial Serbian and Wallachian rule via Hungary's King Sigismund. He created the buffer area (Romania) to ease the Ottoman Empire's encroaching expansion north. The stone walls that were built could not keep the annual Ottoman raids at bay, and many towns were ruled by wealthy criminals that delighted in taking money for minimal protection.

The flashback came as swiftly as the air went rushing out of her lungs.

Irina remembered the exact moment where this had all begun, and she silently mourned her lack of courage and strength to withstand a ludicrous idea of an idiot.

It was one year and four days ago to this very day that she had trusted, hoped and possibly even believed that life would turn out differently for her.

'Who is the idiot now?' she thought as warning bells went off in her brain because of her inability to draw in any air.

~~~

'How in the hell did I end up with this senseless, stupid, irresponsible man?' she thought to herself, fending off waves of disappointment.

She shook her head in dismay at her husband; he sat across their wooden table in their dilapidated little farm house on the outskirts of a small town, set back from a country road. A house that nobody could find.

Her husband had done a great job at running their name into the ground. They had tried to live life playing by the rules but every time they had, it always ended up worse for them.

Growing up, both of them had been very poor, traveling from town to town with their parents; families in a gypsy train.

Neither one of them had wanted that nomadic lifestyle and they had run away from it, together, when they were both fifteen.

He had promised Irina the world and a beautiful home, with flowers and trees that would be their own.

"We will be the most loved couple in the area. Look at us! We are beautiful people. How could fortune not smile upon us?"

For all of his talk, they had both felt they were destined for something great, something beautiful; much more than their parent's gypsy lifestyle.

She had believed every word he spoke and had followed him on most of his schemes. But time had elapsed and this was a dangerous game he was playing today.

~~~

"You did what?" Irina asked, perplexed by his blasé attitude.

"I borrowed money from the Fitz's so that we could start that business we have talked about for ages. We do not have to pay them back for one whole year. It was only a small loan anyway. What do you care?" her husband answered smugly.

"The Fitz's?!" she screeched. "Do you understand what they will do to us if you don't pay them back?!"

"But we will pay them back. What are you talking about? People, especially women, want to buy things. They want their fortunes read, their love lives fixed, love potions handed to them, anything that will help them catch their men. We talked about all of this. We agreed! You said it was a great idea. Now we just need to rent one of the small rooms in town and get a sign painted: Madame J'ador's Fortune Telling. It will be magnificent!"

"First of all," she ground out with her jaw clenched so that she wouldn't hit him, "We barely hashed out the idea for this business. Secondly, there are only a handful of people in that town who will be loyal customers. Everyone else is turning into religious parrots or fighting over scraps from the Church's table. Why would you not talk to me about this before you took a loan from those people?"

"Why do you even care? I will be the one they come after for payment," he replied with a shrug.

Irina smacked her forehead with impatience. "Are you an idiot? If this business should fail, or there are not enough clients, or whatever happens, we will still have to pay them back... Come hell or high water! You know what they did to the last family that could not pay them."

His eyes went wide because he had forgotten. The entire family and even the in-laws, burned alive in their homes, one by one, in the dead of night with no witnesses and no survivors.

Letting out an anguished sigh, she rose from the table. Irina would have to make this business work. There was nothing else she could do; there was no way to pay the loan back once it was received as there was interest accruing on it from the moment he had accepted it.

The other businesses had failed; the farm, the sewing, the washing - all founded on her relentless labor. But he did not have a head for business, which meant she had to keep track of the monies and supplies, and she was too tired after all her effort and toiling to try to supervise what he was doing with the money as well.

During these business trials, he would head off during the day on their horse, searching for a job of any kind. After he had quit (or been fired, depending on who one asked) due to the employer being too mean or too harsh or the many other excuses she was sick of hearing, he would sneak off to drink.

The drink had been a problem for him, ever since he had first tried it from a stranger who passed through their land four years ago. At first, he had become deathly sick from it. Recently, he would seek it out no matter where they were.

Now he was a secret drinker. He tried to hide how much he drank from her; as if she could not smell it on his breath. Claiming he could quit at any time, the maximum number of days he could go before succumbing to the drink was twelve. She knew; she had counted and then cried herself to sleep as reality hit home that he was a drunk.

She would have suggested they start making alcohol and selling it if she could guarantee he would not drink it all before they could sell it! It would have been a great business if he did not have this drinking problem. Everybody drank, even the Christian priests.

Peeking at Irina from his seat, he tried to look bashful, as if his forgetfulness was not a problem. As if borrowing money from one of the most blood-thirsty families in the entire country was a non-issue.

Shaking her head at him, she threw her dinner bowl at his head. Moving his head at the last second, he dodged the wooden bowl and it hit the wall behind him.

He laughed and then smiled his charming, come hither smile; the one he knew she could not resist. As he crooked his finger at her, she smiled back at him through her vexation. She tried to rebuff him but his pull on her body was too much for her to resist, and she sauntered towards him with her hips swaying.

Once she had reached him, he put his arms around her and her exasperation vanished when he leaned down to kiss her. He kissed her so firmly that it knocked the air out of her lungs.

The one thing that had not gone away in these past six years was their chemistry. He could still make her shudder even when she wanted to murder him.

As he leisurely removed her first layer of clothing, she shook the thoughts of gloom and doom out of her mind. Conceivably their luck was changing. She would make the fortune telling work. It could be profitable if done competently.

Perhaps he was not the dumbest man she had ever encountered. Irina could only hope.

~~~

The tarot business actually went smoothly. People came from miles around to get their love potions or fortunes told.

It surprised Irina that many of her returning customers were men. They seemed the most obsessed with their futures: would they be rich, would they find and marry a beautiful woman, would their business be prosperous, would their wife die early so they could marry someone else, would their children make suitable matches or gain parcels of land with the marriages. These were her most common questions.

But the men were the most covert about it, along with the most respectful. If she told a man what she saw (a skill she had learned from her mother), she also said this is not his fate if he decided to take actions to change it.

When Irina said that same line to a woman, the woman would whine and cry, and then storm out of the building. They would return asking her how they could change it and what they needed to do, and she would charge them more for not being able to use their own brains or hearts to lead them to where they desired to go.

At least most of the men never asked Irina to hold their hand and make step by step plans for them.

If only women were that easy. Instead, they wanted fail-safe options on how to rope a man in, or not to have children, or to have more children, and other domestic issues.

She learned to start telling some of the women what they wanted to hear after a while. It was simpler this way and did not complicate everything. A few of these women were not good people and the less Irina had to be around them, the better it would be for her.

Knowing that she had received many worthwhile lessons from her mother and grandmother around the reading of the tarot cards (which had taken her an entire two weeks to paint) and the telling of another's future using body clues, information, and lines on their hands mixed in with a bits of guidance from her own intuitive emotions and reactions, she was creating quite the sensation as a gifted fortune teller.

This fact should not have surprised Irina, but it did. She had run away from this part of her past life, refusing to be that gypsy woman as her mother had been. The gifts she had for the cards as well as the fortunes were nothing to be laughed at. Nine out of ten times she was correct.

Straightening up her dress and pushing stray hairs back so that she looked proper, she waited on her next client.

~~~

Glancing around the room, it was a beautiful space to tell fortunes. Much better than the rickety wooden cart she had seen fortunes told in while growing up. The inside of that cart had been somewhat shabby and confining.

Her room and office was a luxurious space with a thick dark blue curtain hanging down to block the doorway and the entrance, creating a feeling of peace and separation from the outside world. There was a large painting of a nature scene on a piece of wood that allowed the viewer to feel at one with the world.

Candles and stones were everywhere with a few other various pieces from the countryside that she had picked up including a 'v' shaped piece of tree, a few dried flowers and herbs for aroma, and cushions. One smaller table sat in the corner with three old leather-bound parchments stacked on it. Irina had traded reading a fortune for the parchments with a traveling man selling goods he carried on his back. Having no idea what they said or meant because they were in another language, she nonetheless enjoyed the drawings on a few of the pages.

The main piece of the room was the rounded table with two large wooden chairs presiding over the middle of the room. A smooth piece of yellow cloth draped over the table, with one candle and the tarot cards on it. Plump cushions of green material were tied to the bottom and backs of the chairs so that the people sitting would be relaxed and comfortable.

Pride was gleaming from her face and her eyes sparkled as she examined each and every item in the room. She had picked everything herself and had worked hard to find all of these items. Many of them felt like gifts to her; gifts from nature, from earth, from her ancestors.

Speaking of ancestors, Irina felt as if she was a changed woman. Her purpose in life was clear to her now; she would help those that she could and be as positive as possible for those she could not help. Her gift of sight would guide those who took action onto a better path or at least a more enjoyable one. Remembering who she had been last year, she said a quick prayer of thanks and continued to wait for her client.

Her mother had only let Irina read tarot cards when her grandmother was ill. She looked at the tarot deck from her cushioned chair and thought longingly of them both. 'If they could see me now, they would be proud,' she thought.

~~~

The front door opened and shut swiftly, and Irina heard boots darting towards her. Someone was coming into the tarot card reading area. The curtains spread wide and her husband came scurrying to her side.

"What are you doing here? I have a client soon," she snapped out in irritation.

"Shush. You must come with me. We have to leave. Now," her husband rapidly commanded, out of breath while sweat beads ran down his face.

"What are you talking about? Have you been drinking again? I have a paying client who is going to be here any moment and you need to leave."

"No, Irina, listen to me!" he yelled as he grabbed her arm, jerking her up out of her chair. "The Fitz's are going to come for us and we need to leave now."

"Are you insane? We have been paying them back every month!"

His head could not have sunk down any lower on his neck if she had knocked him with a frying pan. He could not look her directly in the eyes and his tongue darted out of his mouth to lick his bottom lip, a clear sign of his nerves.

"What did you do?!" Irina screamed at him and pushed him as hard as she could.

"Stop! We have to go. I will explain on the way out!" he exclaimed, trying to grab her arm again.

She sidestepped away from him. "I am not leaving! I finally feel that I am doing some good and I feel like a completely new person. You go and I will figure it out with the Fitz's. You always have been a coward! Run like the scared weasel you are!"

"You do not understand! They will kill you just to get to me – it does not matter if I leave or not. Please, now is not the time to be stubborn. I need you to trust me."

Irina started laughing hysterically. "Trust you? TRUST YOU!!!" her voice swelling into a fever pitch. "All I have ever done is trust you and yet time and time again, you somehow make life worse for me. You lead me down into the depths of despair and all I have left to show for it are the scars on my heart and a worn-out, lackluster face, not to mention a wretched existence with you as my husband."

"Please, Irina, my love. I am sorry. I have learned my lesson but we must go if we are going to outrun them. I have packed everything we need and the horses are out in back. We can sneak out the back window."

Pushing past him since she had no option, Irina raced towards the back kitchenette room with a window. Opening it swiftly she climbed out of it. Rushing towards the horses, she glanced back at him as she picked up her skirts.

Saying nothing, he helped her up onto the smaller horse. They had one saddle and it was on his very large horse, with everything tied to the saddle. She could only pray that there was enough food and money in there to get them to the next place.

They needed to leave the country straightaway. There was no other option. He had finally gone past the point of no return and she was going to pay the price with him.

There was nothing she could do about it.

As their horses galloped into the sunset, there was a great deal of pain in her expression. Currently, they were in unknown territory and she hoped that they had a far enough lead on the Fitz's to avoid an excruciating death.

~~~

Five days.

They had been riding hard for five long days. Irina could not feel her backside anymore and her legs barely held her when she slid off the horse each night.

Resting as much as they could and giving the horses more food to recover quickly from the hard rides, they kept pressing on. From what she could, tell they were almost to the border. They both knew there was a large stone wall at the border to the south. The peoples of the south did not want the northerners on their lands and were sick of the thieving and warring; thus, they had built a massive wall to keep the intruders out.

Once she and Codrin made it to the wall and over it, they would be able to hide easier. However, the question would be how could they get over the wall?

That would be an issue to think about once they got to the wall. Most likely, it was another day or two away. If they were in luck, it would be sooner.

Irina still could not believe what her husband had done. How could she have trusted him? She should have known that Codrin would never change.

After hearing his story, she had decided that she would quietly part ways with him while he was sleeping one night once they were over the wall. She could no longer tie herself to his miserable, wearisome ways. There was no way she would die next to this senseless and irresponsible man.

He had finally let it all out on the third night when they had stopped to eat and sleep. The first few days and nights they did not speak at all; only fell into an exhausted slumber far away from each other covered in blankets. They did not dare to make a fire. Fires were beacons to anyone hunting them and they needed as much safety as they could get.

"I did not mean for this to happen," he said somberly.

"You never mean for it to happen, but it always happens," she replied quietly.

Irina could see his hands shaking, not from remorse but from the lack of alcohol. There was no pity left in her. She was too tired for pity and absolutely repulsed by his frequent misfortunes.

Why had she never told his future? Perhaps she had been too scared of what it would have revealed. She did not know how to read her own or else she could have avoided this.

Maybe.

"I am sorry, you must know that. Everything was going so well for us. You were happy with your business and I was feeling on top of the world because, finally, one of my ideas was good. And that is where it should have ended. But I was arrogant. I decided that since my luck had changed, I would see if I could turn it into something more."

He paused and took a deep breath. Not even daring to look at her, he kept his eyes fixed on the ground.

"I wanted to show you that I could win and be the charming man I used to be. While everything was going so well in your fortune telling, I wanted to have extra money to throw around so that we could get anything we wanted. Fix up the house, go on a trip, anything."

Staying silent, she stared at him. Irina knew where this was going. Codrin would never grow up. He was always trying to impress others, to prove himself to be something he never could be because he had simply never outgrown childhood. He was stuck in the emotional state of a child, hoping that mommy and daddy would say 'good job' and give him a pat on the back with a look of tender pride on their faces.

"I was talking with that hired hand of the Fitz's, Henric, and he told me about a card game they were going to have the following evening. I knew you would be working late so I decided it would all work out. There was no way I could lose. I had only had one drink when I asked Henric to get me a spot in the game," he said with the same sense of delusion he had used to convince himself.

"He told me not to because he truly did not want me to be beholden to the Fitz's any more than I already was. I told him not to worry about me, and just get me in. Once I had won, I would give Henric some of the money for getting me a seat at the table. After much persuasion, he finally agreed and let me know on the following morning that I had a spot in the game."

Tampering down her murderous rage at his infantile thought process, she decided to keep quiet. Irina knew that not all men were this dumb, as many of her clients were quite intelligent.

Somehow, she had ended up with this stunted man-boy, paying back his sins out of her own hard work and determination. Why had she tied herself to him? She was smart enough to make her own way in the world.

Irina should have left Codrin long ago, but their childhood love had kept her rooted next to him, making her feel that she owed him her life despite her unhappiness and his ineptitude.

When she knew he would never change, she should have run fast and far away from him. He was bad news and he was followed by defeat; she saw that now. That meant he would never rise above, and he would always drown anyone tied to him in poverty and misery.

She would leave him as soon as they made it over the wall. Parting ways would be best for both of them.

It is what Irina would advise any of her clients to do if they had such a man in their lives.

Codrin continued, "I did not take a drink before the game that day and I did not have one while I played. I could hear you telling me that the drink has me making foolish decisions and taking risks that do not make sense, so I refrained. After the third round, it was just me against one Fitz brother and one wealthy merchant from out of town."

He smiled at her then, as if she should be proud of his ability to make it to the fourth round. She wanted to smack him and yell, "Wake up!" but Irina held her peace. Glowering at him until he started to fidget, she nodded her head for him to continue.

"They cheated. I do not know how but they cheated. They were in on it together and somehow they took all of the money I had made in the games prior. I had made enough for both of us to enjoy and pay back the Fitz's that day. Instead, they cheated me."

Letting out an exasperated groan, she rolled her eyes. It was always somebody else's fault. Never his. He never took responsibility for his actions, or the lack of them. Blaming everyone else until he was blue in the face was his character.

Irina had thought it simply a character flaw that he would outgrow. Now she knew it was merely who he was and that he did not want to change.

"No, really Irina, they cheated me. I know I have blamed everyone else before, but they really did. Everyone in the room watching knew it too. I glanced around the room and saw the pity on the other player's faces. I had been swindled and there was nothing I could do about it. I wanted to yell at them and kill them. Instead, I laid down my cards and said 'good game' and I even shook their stupid hands."

"Are you telling me that we ran away because you were cheated out of a card game?" she asked softly.

"No! That is not what happened. Or, that is not all of it. I came home and went to lay next to you, and waking up the next day determined to say something to the Fitz's mother. After all, she is the one who truly leads them. You had already left for work by the time I was ready to get up. I did not start walking towards the Fitz house until after I had eaten lunch. But I did not even make it to them. On my way there, luckily I ran into Henric. He had been searching for me discreetly all morning.

Grabbing my horse's lead, he led me off into the woods away from the main road. He found a secluded spot and dismounted. There Henric told me in a whisper that he had overheard a meeting between the Fitz brothers and their mother that morning as he was heading in to report for duty.

They were talking about the card game and laughing at the beating they gave me. Henric told me that he was getting ready to turn to leave but then one of the sons said, 'We should just kill him already. Even if he pays back his loan, I want his woman for myself. She is cleaning up nicely these days and her business is making quite a tidy profit that I would not mind having a piece of.'

After the laughter had died down, the mother asked how much they had tricked me out of. 'All of the loan and more. Enough for us to not even notice that he is gone. He is a drunk anyways. I am sure his woman would be happy to have him gone. She does all of the hard work in that household.'

The mother agreed and said, 'Kill him when and however you see fit. I leave it up to you. However, his wife is to be left alone. She had no part in the loan or the repayment of it even though she is the one repaying it to save him. And I will be the one that goes and speaks with her about her business, none of you. If she wants our protection, she will gladly pay for it.'

'Yes, mama,' they all agreed and then she declared that the meeting was over. Henric took the opportunity to loudly walk up to the door, knock and report his findings and get his duties for the day from the mother.

We consider each other friends and that is why he warned me. Henric has helped me out and I have helped him out before. He is probably my only friend…besides you of course, Irina."

~~~

All she could do was stare at him in perplexed disbelief.

Irina did not want Codrin to die, yet the Fitz family had offered her a way to make a free, new life without him. He could have run away by himself and left her to deal with them!

His selfishness and not wanting to give her up, or his pride, would not let him leave her. He could have told her this in her office and she would have told him to go on without her.

She wanted to scream and cry at the same time. Her life would have been her own! So what? Pay the Fitz's a bit of money each month for protection and one of the brothers liked her. She could have dealt with those issues. What she could not deal with was her husband's deceit.

This was his last act of selfishness that she would ever allow. She could stand him no longer. Any love Irina had once felt for him was completely gone now.

Her fury started making her hands shake and she knew her body agreed with her decision. With the anger she felt right now, she might kill him herself and head back to the town.

All of her things were still there. Her office, her curtains, her dresses, her things that she had gotten with her own hands; it was all there.

And to go forward with nothing. They had nothing. Was there even any money in that bag?

"When you say you lost it all in the card game, do you mean that we have nothing with which to build a new life upon? There is no money in that bag of goods or in your pocket?" Irina questioned him.

He hung his head.

"No, there is nothing left. Only a few coins with which we can buy some food and lodging for a few days but that is all."

Rage shot through her again, mixed with a healthy dose of disgust.

"And you thought it was better to drag me along on this horrible journey than to simply let me stay there and live my life. You know that I can take care of myself!" she said heavily, her voice shaking with anger.

"But they might have raped you or killed you or made you their slave. You never know with them!" he declared as if he had saved her.

"YOU!" Irina screamed at him. "You are worse than the devil himself. You are the most vile, despicable human being I have ever known. Not only do you drown yourself and your dreams, you drown mine. You have made me a slave to your idiocy and self-absorption. I could have been free!"

Distress marred his charming face and his eyes watered. Codrin opened his mouth but had no words.

"You do not care about me, you only care about yourself. Stop acting as if you saved me from anything. You saved yourself and have dragged me along with you only because I am your wife - not to save me…"

"I will be the one to work in the new town we settle in. I will be the one to bring in the food and the money. I will be the one who does it all, as usual," she exclaimed.

"You are a worthless child, incapable of loving anyone but himself. I should have left you long ago when I first realized this!" Irina shrieked at him, disdain dripping from her words, wounding him deeply with her contempt.

He swayed backwards as if she had hit him. He sighed and declared, "But I wanted to save you! That was my only thought."

"Stop lying! You can lie to yourself but you cannot lie to me. I know who and what you are. You are a coward only capable of loving himself. You have ruined my life for the last time," she said.

"What does that mean?" Codrin whispered at her.

"That means that as soon as we get over that wall, you go your way and I will go mine. I want nothing to do with you ever again. I have had enough of you." With that, Irina turned her back on him and sat facing the other way to not have to look at him.

He started crying and blubbering but it fell on deaf ears. She was no longer attached to him in any way. Her survival instincts had kicked in and she knew she would face certain death if she stayed by his side.

His battles were not hers and they never had been. He needed to face his demons on his own.

~~~

Irina could see the wall, but they needed to rest. They had been riding relentlessly all day and had not stopped for the usual water break for the horses.

They slowed down and finally stopped not far from the wall. It was high. A man standing on top of his horse would be able to jump up on it.

"How will both of us get over the wall," she asked him.

He pondered her question as he fed the horses.

"You will hold my horse still as I stand on his back. After I am up, I will reach down to grab you up. But we will not know until we ride up next to it. From this position, it seems doable."

"You do not think we would do better to fashion a ladder of sorts that we can pull with us once we are on top?"

"We do not have the time, my dear. They must be getting close," he sighed.

"They are not after me, so it is only you who needs to get over the wall. I can say that you took me against my will," she said.

"You would do that? Why do you want to leave me? Have I not always loved you? Am I not the one that got us away from our families and being a gypsy to living in a town?" he agonized.

"Do not try to persuade me that you are the reason I am alive. You are the reason I am close to death and being chased by murderers. You are the worst thing that has ever happened to me," she answered harshly.

He sighed again. Codrin knew that her mind was made up, and although it pained him, he would let her go. She would make sure of that.

After all, Irina was the strongest person he knew.

Reaching into the bag of goods, he pulled out the last of the bread and cheese. They had a few more apples and some nuts left. They would need to find a town quickly.

Neither one of them knew what lay beyond the wall but there had to be a town not too far from it or else someone would not have built the wall in this location.

She thought tosuggest that they ride along it for miles, seeking the end of it. Yet, what if they had built it to completely border their entire country to the south? Here was as good a place as any to jump over it.

And since there had not been any rain behind them, their tracks were easy to follow. She had prayed for rain to give them more time but nothing had happened.

Chewing the last mouthful of her tiny portion of the bread and cheese, she contemplated their predicament. They possibly had one full day on the Fitz's. Thinking that they had any more would be folly. One of the brothers was also an excellent tracker. There was no use thinking any more about this. Irina needed rest.

Falling asleep after finally getting comfortable, she slept better than she had on previous evenings knowing that they were close to escaping over the wall, and she was one step closer to total freedom from her husband.

Perhaps we will fashion that ladder, she thought as she drifted off to sleep, exhausted from the riding and emotions. Irina wrapped her blanket tightly around her and lay down to sleep. His sobs lulled her to sleep more quickly than she expected.

~~~

Feeling a hasty kick against her foot, she woke up startled.

"Move it! We have to go. I can feel the ground shaking with hooves. It's them," her husband yelled as he threw a backpack over his shoulder.

Irina jumped up and threw her blanket into the bag. He untied her horse and hoisted her up onto it. Rushing to his own already saddled horse, he jumped up on him and they took off at a gallop towards the wall.

Looking behind her, she could see the Fitz brothers off in the distance, a faraway dot on the horizon. It would take the hunters a while to reach the wall.

Her heart thundering in her chest and her breathing shallow, she dismounted quickly as her horse whinnied and ran off. Her own nervous energy had most likely been felt by the horse and scared it off.

She grabbed the reins of Codrin's horse as he stood up on its back. He was able to place his hands on top of the wall and jump up. Once he had thrown the bag over, he looked back down at her.

She was struggling to mount his horse. Breathing deeply, she pulled herself up into the saddle. She tried to calm herself so that the horse would remain calm and not bolt as she stood up.

Codrin spoke gently to the horse, "Steady now, we need you to stay still, old buddy."

The horse seemed to calm down as Codrin continued to speak to it, trying to keep the horse standing firm.

Placing her feet flat on the saddle, Irina slowly started to straighten her knees to stand up, grabbing the wall. But even with her husband reaching down with one hand, she would have to jump to grab his hand and if she missed, she would land on the horse and the horse would bolt.

She had to get it right the first time.

Hearing the pounding of hooves beating into the earth, she knew the riders were getting closer. The Fitz's were almost upon her. Her hands started to sweat and she felt her face getting damp.

"It's alright, sweetheart. Just jump. I will catch you. Take a deep breath and jump!"

She closed her eyes and took a deep breath to still her heart. She could do this. Codrin would catch her. As short in stature as she was, he would catch her and haul her up.

Opening her eyes, she looked up at him, raised her right arm, took a deep inhale while bending her knees and jumped up towards her husband.

Her eyes widened in horror as her fingers missed his hand by a mere fraction.

"Noooo!" Codrin yelled and the horse bolted.

Irina fell hard onto the ground and the air left her lungs.

She could not breathe.

"Get up, sweetheart. Get up, Irina. The horse is right there. Try it again!"

As she tried to work air into her lungs so that she could move, one of the Fitz men ran his horse right up next to her. Grabbing Irina from the ground and pushing her up against the wall, he held her throat tightly with one hand as he removed a knife from his belt with his other hand.

"Since you dragged her into your foolish escape, you will get to watch her die," the Fitz brother yelled up to her husband and then started laughing as tears ran down her face.

"NOOOOO!" she heard Codrin bellow as she swung her head to look up into the crazed eyes of the Fitz brother that held her.

He looked completely insane and she was sure she had never seen him before. He was like a wild animal that had been let loose on the public without any warning, destroying anyone in his path who would try to put him back into his prison.

Her brain was screaming at her lack of air and her eyes started to look wildly about for help.

Before the other brothers on horseback could reach the crazy one, he slit her throat and pushed her away like a discarded handkerchief.

Irina grabbed at her neck, trying to keep the blood from pouring out of her, as she fell to her knees. Tears streamed down her face as she fell completely flat onto the dry soil.

Dying on the ground, she looked up at the sky; it had started to rain!

'Too late. It was all too late,' she thought as her body convulsed one last time.

A few lessons learned in this lifetime:

No self-esteem in addition to a marriage in her teens led to knowing she deserved better than her marriage and her alcoholic husband; but she didn't wake up or leave until it was too late. She had finally found her calling yet she had bet on someone else above her own self. She lived her life hoping it would all work out while doing nothing to help herself. However, she did not take control of her life and died with regret and resentment which followed into the next lifetime.

Chapter 8

The Village Healer

839 CE

Serbia was a territory constantly being invaded by Bulgaria, although many of the tribes were united under Vlastimir. Many small towns consisted of trading farm goods and simple items. Life was hard but uncomplicated. War did not touch the villages near the forests due to the cities hoarding the wealth and trade goods. Myth and superstition, as well as healing from ancient remedies and knowledge, were stronger than ever, despite the Catholic Church's reach.

She looked around her hut with a furrowed brow. For years there had been nothing re-arranged, nothing out of place. Every item had its use. Herbs hung everywhere in her earthen hut. A fireplace hung in the corner. As far as huts went, it was rather large. Her long-dead husband had seen to that.

~~~

Digging the hut into the side of a hill next to a forest had been the best idea he ever had, god love him. He was not too much on the bright side, but he was a hard worker and he had loved her in his way. Their time together had been brief; however, she was grateful to him.

Not long after their speedy courtship of two months and then their marriage shortly thereafter, she had fallen pregnant. He decided to add on a few more rooms into the earthen mound which meant there was dirt everywhere during the first few months of their marriage.

He had wanted a lot of children and Jana would shrug when he mentioned it, for she had only wanted out of her parent's horribly overcrowded dwelling full of overbearing, guilt-ridden and toxic family members.

Her mother, Sanja, had been constantly pregnant since Jana was a small child and there seemed to be an ebb of life force within her mother following each childbirth. Sanja was now a shell of the cheerful woman she used to be. Jana did not wish to be anything like that.

If they had children or not, she did not care one way or the other. But he would bring it up almost every day.

She would only sigh as she looked down, continuing to mix her herbs as he carried on about their numerous children he wanted but did not have yet. Afterwards, these herbal concoctions would be added to little sachets and pots of healing creams, ointments, and elixirs for paying neighbors and kin.

~~~

It was a few days after they had spoken (well, while he had spoken) on this subject for the twentieth time that Jana had discovered she was pregnant. The feeling of horror and excitement had risen simultaneously within her.

Yet there was also happiness bubbling up within her, for this child was hers and would belong to her. She would teach her child all she knew and love her deeply, and there would never be any question as to why she was born.

It was going to be a girl; she had known it from the moment she felt she was pregnant. Perhaps she will give birth to a lineage that will work in a castle or a court, mixing herbs for queens and kings. That would be nice to be provided for like that, she thought.

However, that day felt as if it was ages ago.

Disappointment had raged throughout her body when her husband had died chopping wood out their front door; she had been almost nine months pregnant with a round and massive belly that threatened to burst at any time.

Glancing at the fireplace with its shelves filled with jars and the dirt roof, she leaned back and stretched, inhaling the strong smell of earth and herbs. Her kitchen area was also the main room of the house and she loved being able to access all her potions and heating elements in one area.

Her husband's face had faded from her memories all of those years ago, along with all of the emotions she had felt towards him, soon after his untimely death.

Jana's thoughts wandered back to that time; she had been seated in this very kitchen mixing herbs when she heard him holler with a short, pained cry. She had yelled his name two times and neither had gotten a response.

A shiver passed over her body as she waddled outside, clutching her lower belly with her right hand in a protective manner. Slowly making her way to where he lay dead by the wood pile with half of the log chopped, she said a peaceful prayer, asking his soul to find rest and its way to the other side lovingly.

Then her body started to shake as she grasped what had happened. There were no tears streaming down her face, for she did not love him as a person loves their lover. The shaking was from the realization that she was all alone in this earthen hut, a month or less away from having her baby with no neighbors or friends for miles, and family that came around once every few months, if that.

She would be having this baby alone unless someone showed up miraculously.

~~~

"And it's about to be winter," Jana said aloud as she looked at the half-chopped log. "He could have at least chopped the rest of the log before he keeled over!" she exclaimed.

How was she going to chop a log in her current state? She'd end up giving birth on the log pile. Not the most comforting thought.

Nor was the fact that she knew what childbirth entailed and she would have to boil water while doing everything herself. Hopefully the pain reducing herbs would work on her and ease the birthing pains but that was not guaranteed. Every woman is different.

Staring down at his body, she nudged it with her foot. She really wanted to kick him to release some of the fury she felt towards his premature death.

She raised her face up towards the sky and howled instead, releasing all of the anger and frustration in a lengthy wail. Feeling better, she looked down at his body.

"Looks as if I will be out here chopping wood in the middle of winter with a baby attached to me," she said to him. "Thank you for all of your help in making this child-bearing journey a real joy," she sarcastically remarked with a smile.

Jana giggled at that.

~~~

Her dream of having only loving thoughts as the baby came into the world went up in flames. Fighting for survival through the depths of winter while trying to recuperate her body from the extremities of childbirth would be testing to say the least. If she made it through the next few months along with the baby, she could endure anything.

"At some point, someone will come visiting this winter," she declared with a hopeful countenance.

Family and friends would come to see about the baby, or someone seeking a cure for some winter ailment or disease would find their way to her hut.

Despite her youthfulness, Jana had developed a reputation as a healer, though most people would only come to her as a last resort.

The old healer who lived in the village ten miles from her had killed more people than he had helped or cured, yet people still went to see him first. If they didn't like his fees for a potion, advice or prediction, and after they had tried to heal whatever they suffered from by themselves or from a family remedy, they would come to see her.

However, nobody came that winter.

It was the worst winter she could remember, with snows piling up and storm after storm. If it wasn't snowing, it was raining and if it wasn't raining, it was hailing. Trees could be heard falling down in the forest as she wearily dragged in firewood that she stored in the half-finished children's room, along with the extra food and herbs she had dried for the winter.

The baby's room, which he had finished, was being used to hold the goat. He had never finished building the goat a shelter for the winter and she couldn't go outside to find it while she was this pregnant. The chickens had their coop and she had put plenty of food out there yesterday; enough to last for a few days. They would need to be fed by the fourth day or they would die. She needed their eggs to stay healthy and make the baby strong. An egg a day makes a strong and healthy baby, her grandmother always advised.

She cursed her dead husband in a scream, while she squatted down, giving birth over a basin of warm water that was slowly getting mixed with fluids falling from her insides. Squatting activated the body to push out what was ready to come out.

Holding onto chairs on either side of her arms, she willed the baby to come out. She could not keep squatting like this as she had no assistance; her body was exhausted and hungry, and the fire was roaring as sweat rolled down her face and back.

The baby would come out soon. She must.

After ten or so minutes of squatting, she felt as if her legs would cramp up. The pain was lessened by the herbs she had drunk as soon as her water had broken.

Everything was ready beside her; a cot for her to sleep and cuddle with the baby, large animal fur blankets, plenty of firewood, water to drink, water to bathe, numerous cloths and a few blankets for the baby, some bread and dried fruit and cheese, and boiled eggs kept covered in a pot. There was also a pot of chicken and herb soup she had made that would help her keep her strength up.

A knife was by the fire to sterilize it in the flames, and once the baby was delivered, at peace and rested for a few hours, she would use the knife to cut the cord away from the afterbirth. Three ointments, an elixir and two herb mixtures were on the ground further away just in case there were complications.

She felt ready.

Having nobody here to help her in the midst of this chaotic life-giving dance, which was as ancient as time itself, was far less than ideal. Yet many women had delivered their own children all alone.

"I can do this on my own," Jana whispered to herself. The pain would not swallow her into oblivion, she was strong.

Her legs started to shake. She raised her head up towards the earthen ceiling and screamed, "God or gods or whoever is there, I command you to release this baby from my body and onto this earth. She is ready to come out now!"

One minute later, while trying to control her breathing as the pain wracked her entire being, the baby poured out of her and into the basin of water. Grabbing the baby up out of the water, she saw that her eyes were open but no sound was coming out of her little mouth.

~~~

Jana gently massaged her baby's chest, clearing her eyes and mouth, and examined her tiny body for abnormalities. There were none; and still, the baby gazed at her with wide, dark eyes. Perhaps the baby was contemplating her new life, Jana thought.

She held the baby close to her for warmth as she continued squatting over the basin. The afterbirth came out not long after she had focused on it, willing it out of her body quickly as well. The baby did not cry or move, despite her body responding to the removal of that which was no longer needed.

Glancing down at her daughter, she felt pure love course through her veins; possibly for the first time in her entire life, if she was being honest with herself. She looked to be so wise!

"You are mine, little girl. I am so glad you are mine. Thank you for coming out so quickly," she said joyfully. After gently cleaning the baby off, she wrapped her in a blanket and held her next to her breast. The baby's eyes started to blink, as if heavy with weight, and soon she fell asleep without eating or crying.

"Well then... I shall call you Sofija." the healer whispered, and moved the basin closer towards the cot so that she could place the baby on it. There were vital properties within the cord and sac that the baby needed, thus it must stay attached as long as possible.

Ensuring the baby slept, she turned to a different bucket of water near the fire so that she could clean herself off.

~~~

As the child grew, so did Jana's reputation as a healer.

She had memorized all of her recipes, and would change or perfect them as needed. People came from all over to be healed by her because she was the most knowledgeable healer for many miles. They also came because she had, as well, earned a reputation of correcting others' mistakes.

Her potions seemed to heal people faster, and every one of them was made with love for the specific patient she was treating; that was how she was able to heal and harmonize with their soul. They needed the love that went into the recipe as much as the medicine she gave them.

People would pay her with food or coin, or sometimes with their hard labor if she needed anything fixed around her small plot of land; for she had refused to get married again, as was expected of her.

Jana was aware that she was a short, small woman raising her child alone near a forest. This was simply how she enjoyed her life and she knew that her mission was to heal others and raise Sofija with love.

Some of her male patients had fancied themselves in love with her and would hang about her hut for a while or randomly show up with gifts of wild flowers, grains or meat.

Always appreciative of the help, she would direct them to the single women in the village that she knew of, or other widows. Most people tended to be lonely, but she was far from that. Her daughter kept her smiling and active.

~~~

When Sofija turned twelve, Jana formally initiated her as a healer. She had taught her daughter everything she knew, and Sofija's inquisitive mind had produced new potions and creams.

They hunted for different herbs in the forest together and had grown an extensive herb garden for those herbs that could be grown in a domesticated manner. The garden near their house supplied more than enough of the ingredients they needed, and this is where they spent most of their time, either digging in the ground, multiplying certain seedlings, or sitting outside by a terrace, which had been added to the now completed home, the rooms that were now furnished thanks to the healing goods and services she was able to trade with.

Near their home they also had available to them multiple unused plots of land, which they would use for composting, or the germinating of new trees, starchy edibles, mushrooms, or moon magic. That meant less time trekking in the woods, and more time for relaxation and fun.

It would still be a few years before Jana would allow her daughter to walk to town alone, but she enjoyed giving her the freedom of dreaming in the forest or lying in the grass with her eyes closed while the sun beat down on her somewhat childish frame.

Sofija was not a tall girl and had most likely reached her full height at age twelve. Jana frowned slightly at this thought.

She was a sensitive girl and highly capable of knowing what ailed people before they even spoke. Sofija's skills far surpassed Jana's, who helped her cultivate them as far as she could.

There was no other healer to send Sofija to for more knowledge or learning, at least nobody that was within fifty miles of them. Thus, Jana was determined to do her best and keep her daughter close since most people would not understand her abilities or her unique sensitivity and power.

Sofija would cry for days if one of the chickens died or she found a dead bird in the forest. She had been empathetic like that since she was a toddler.

But she would protect her daughter as long as she could. There was always news of strangers coming or foreign kings searching for expert healers; this led Jana to keep a low profile and to hope that her reputation remained local. Once Sofija took over her healing practice, Jana knew it could lead to a different life for her daughter altogether.

Only time would tell.

~~~

Six happy years later, Sofija told Jana about the man she loved, Andrej. He was five years Sofija's senior, and had visited them quite often over the last few years.

Of course, Jana liked this man. He had been nothing but respectful and funny, making them both laugh. He was from a long line of farmers and horse breeders, and even sold horses to the wealthy traders. Andrej also fixed various issues around the house and small farm. The summer before Sofija's eighteenth birthday, Andrej had helped the wanderer build a barn for their animals.

The wanderer, Tadej, had made her small farm his home seven years before this. He was a quiet but large man, and had helped them expand the garden while he looked after their animals and ran errands in the village that had now become a small and bustling, trading town. He kept out of their way so much that Jana forgot about him most of the time.

Tadej had the presence of a mighty warrior running away from something. However, Jana had never asked him about his past and he had never spoken of it. He seemed content sleeping in a room on the top floor of the barn where the hay was kept, and she felt better for having a male close by as her daughter had turned into a beautiful, tiny woman.

Knowing that Sofija would choose to marry her lover, Jana gave her blessing and they married in the summer right before her daughter turned nineteen.

Andrej had purchased land less than a mile away from Jana's earthen hut, knowing that his bride wanted to be close to her mother and continue her own work as a healer.

Most evenings, he would come to meet Sofija and they would share dinner together as a family before the couple left. Tadej always joined these meals and they would talk and chuckle collectively. Andrej would talk about current events in the town while the girls made lists for the following day of elixirs and potions to be made, or patients that needed further examination.

~~~

A few years after her marriage, Sofija gave birth to a girl. She was named Lidija, meaning noble and beautiful. Jana attended this birth which was quick and easy, with the baby making no fuss and no hardship for her mother.

Jana looked at her granddaughter and held her close, saying the same thing she said to her daughter when she was born, "You are mine, little girl. I am so glad you are mine. Thank you for coming out so quickly. I cannot wait to show you all that I know, as I did your mother."

Lidija simply blinked at Jana as if acknowledging and understanding her words.

"You will rest, my beautiful daughter. I am here and will continue to visit every day. I forbid you to come back to work with me for at least two months," Jana told Sofija as she lightly placed the baby into her daughter's arms.

Sofija smiled up at Jana. "Of course, mother. I knew you would say that and I agree. My body will need time to heal and I will enjoy getting to know this little girl. We should probably let my husband into the room before he kicks the door down," she joked.

As the grandmother slowly opened the door, she gestured with her eyes to enter. Andrej came striding in with impatience. Tears streamed down his face as he looked at his wife and his newborn daughter.

Jana quietly closed the door behind her, smiling at the love she felt for her new granddaughter as well as the love she witnessed from the little family within the room.

Love. There was no more important feeling than love. Love could heal people and love could drive people to madness, but a love for one's child was timeless.

~~~

Lidija grew quickly, perhaps fueled by all the love that surrounded her or due to her being from good strong family lineages on both sides. Either way, Jana began showing Lidija the healing arts at the age of two. Her granddaughter had not started speaking yet, but she was an avid learner.

Sofija would make visits into the town to heal people, charging a heavy fee for this service. Due to her prominent reputation, Sofija was the first person people called on or sent a message to when they were sick.

~~~

Thus, Jana had her granddaughter to herself for large portions of time, and this made them both happy. Old people and babies understand each other. Something about being at opposite ends of the timeline make it such a symbiotic relationship. Jana doted on her granddaughter and the child loved watching patients that came to the earthen hut leave, feeling loved and getting their health back.

The earthen hut was the granddaughter's second home and Jana knew Lidija would live here after her death. She told Sofija and Andrej that when she died, the home and small farm would go to her granddaughter. Any money Jana had would go to Lidija as well.

"Mother, you are very kind and generous. She will be told once she is older. Thank you," her daughter said as she rubbed her belly. She was now pregnant with their second child.

"If this child is a boy, then he will take over your farm and house. My first grandbaby must never feel that because she is a woman she will be helpless or homeless unless a man marries her," Jana said with a laugh.

Her daughter had never been helpless or homeless, but Sofija understood the truth behind the sentiment for this was the way of the world they lived in.

She nodded towards her mother as the husband replied, "No matter what happens, it is her choice what she chooses for her life. Healing, living on this farm, getting married…she is from a line of wise women. She will know what is best for her own life."

Both women smiled at Andrej with love. He was a good man who protected his women and provided for them. He never let his mother-in-law go without something she needed, and would also bring Jana small trinkets from town every now and again to remind her that he loved her as a part of his family.

~~~

When Lidija was fourteen, she had surpassed Jana and Sofija in the healing arts. She was born to be a healer, and her dreams were much larger than her two teachers.

"Grandma, I will make our potions and elixirs and creams into a line of goods that are sold not only in our town's goods store, they will be sold in other towns as well."

"Oh really, my child? That seems like a wonderful dream. I hope that you achieve this. You must remember that most of these medicines can only be used for a year or so after they are made. You do not want anybody buying an old remedy or they might become sick from it."

"Yes. I understand and will work out a solution."

"I know you will. I believe in you," the healer said to her granddaughter with a smile.

Jana had gotten older and her hair had turned gray. Her movements were slower and she depended more upon the wanderer to help with the food and herb gardens, as well as other tasks around the farm.

Often Jana would ponder if she would die before Tadej did. That would make it easier on her, she had decided with a laugh. Dragging his dead body to his grave at her age would definitely finish her off, not to mention be an exhausting way to die.

Glancing at her precious granddaughter, Jana kept her thoughts to herself. Her granddaughter's path would be much more interesting than her own. She knew that Lidija would become a famous healer throughout the land and that the king and noble families would want her at court.

All of the jars and pots of healing mixtures would not be able to keep her safe at court. Brooding over this, she speculated if her granddaughter would keep the small farm and hut or reside in a larger town.

"My dear, you are destined for great things. Once your line of healing goods is sold throughout the land, you will be sought after by kings, queens and noblemen. You must follow your heart. It will never lead you astray. Ask your heart what you should do and listen for the answer. Friends will come and go; nevertheless your heart will always remain steadfast and loving towards you. Remember that above all else."

"Thank you, grandmother. You are so wise. I hope one day to be as wise as you," Lidija replied as she slipped her arms around Jana's waist, hugging Jana so hard that she could not continue to grind herbs together in her bowl.

The healer laughed and her granddaughter started laughing. There was so much love and happiness shared between them.

Sofija came into the hut just then, and observing their laughter and hugging, she joined in. She was much smaller than them, so her shorter arms could not fully encircle both of them.

Regardless, the love vibrated within and spilled out of the small hut, filling them all with joy.

~~~

Once the winter had come, the healer knew it was her time to go. This would be her last winter, thank god, Jana said to herself. Winters were the worst as she could not travel to her daughter's house so easily.

Her granddaughter was busy knitting winter gloves and socks for the less fortunate and would keep at it until she had finished fifty pairs. It would most likely take Lidija another two weeks to complete the task.

Her grandson came around a few times each week to see if she needed any errands run or extra work done that the wanderer could not complete. Ivan was a sweet boy but she did not feel as spiritually connected to him as she was to his sister and mother.

Ivan added joy to their lives and had also been an easy child for his mother. He spent most of his time trailing his father and learning about the farm and horses. He was not interested in the healing arts and Jana knew in her heart that healing was not his path.

~~~

Ivan ran into the hut, gave Jana a hug and asked her if she needed anything.

"Tell your mother to come and see me at the latest tomorrow," Jana responded as she hugged him back.

He nodded his head, released her, and darted off into the thick snow.

When Tadej left a pile of logs by the fire later that day, she told him that she would be dead within two days.

"You know that this is your home and you will remain here for as long as you wish. The farm will be my granddaughter's once I am gone. However, I do not think she will remain here for long as she has big dreams and plans," Jana said to him with a wistful smile.

"I want to thank you for giving me a home and love and helping a wayward soul find some level of peace on this earth," he told her. "You have been a sister to me. Please let me know if there is anything I can do for you to ease your ascension."

"That's a lovely word for passing away. There is nothing that needs to be done. My body has said it is time and I know that it is deep down in my soul. I appreciate all that you have done for me as well. You made it safe for me to never have to remarry being in this isolated and desolate area, and provided for me with your skills. I will wait for Sofija to arrive before I depart. If it is a while before my granddaughter moves into the house, perhaps you should stay so that the house does not become empty of life."

"Perhaps I will," Tadej said with a smile and tears in his eyes.

Jana had never seen him shed any tears. She realized she knew mostly nothing about him and that it was not important. Not now, anyway.

If he started to cry, she would start to cry and she did not wish for that. Her life had been happy and long enough, and there was no need for tears.

"I hope you smile more often," she replied as she patted his hand. "No tears, please. I've lived a lengthy and joyful life. Although you are outliving me, I know we will meet again."

He ducked his head to brush a hand over his eyes. "As you wish. We will meet again. I will be close by if you need anything at all. Goodbye, my brave friend," he said lovingly.

Not wanting to cry in front of her as she had asked, Tadej turned swiftly and strode out the door.

Within an hour, her daughter had entered the earthen house. Jana was in bed with a very bright fire roaring in the fireplace.

Upon seeing Jana's face, Sofija knew immediately that her mother was dying. No words needed to be spoken.

Sofija could not imagine her life without her mother; her strong, wise mother who had guided her and her family throughout the years.

Without her mother's influence, she would have become a conventional woman, living a hardened, aimless life, most likely in a loveless relationship and hating her husband. But Jana had given her so much love, so much light, so much healing, that Sofija had married for love and nothing else, and her family reflected that love and more, as her mother had shown her.

Knowing that there was nothing to be done, she pulled up a chair and a blanket next to the bed. Sitting down and getting comfortable, Sofija grabbed her mother's hand.

Jana looked at her. "You have always been my greatest joy and love. Your daughter as well. I know that she will do great things and that you will support her in all, as I have done for you. I hope you continue with your healing work, no matter how renowned your daughter becomes. People need your skills. Try to take an apprentice or two, once Lidija goes off on her own journey. The town still needs the healing we provide; the love that is put into every recipe and remedy. I am so proud of you, my wonderful, beautiful daughter."

"I am so proud of you, mother. Of course, I will continue your work and do what is necessary to pass it on. We are the caregivers of this earth. Hopefully, Lidija will have a daughter to pass it onto as well, but it is more likely that my son will. Lidija does not want children currently; perhaps that will change. Either way, your art will survive to help people. Thank you for all that you have shown us. Thank you for all of the love and faith you have shown me. I will miss our talks and laughter and joy. Most of all, I will miss your hugs and love. You will always be my mother, my best friend and my teacher. There is not a better person I could have been born to, nor a more loving and kind mother."

Sofija squeezed her mother's hand and kissed it with as much love as she could put into a kiss. Tears were flowing down her face as she looked into Jana's eyes.

Despite trying to not shed tears, Jana started to softly cry.

"I am crying, not because I am dying, but because you were the best daughter and greatest gift a mother could ask for. You were the easiest baby, as if you knew that I was all alone giving birth to you and living on this farm unaided for the first few months of winter. You made my life fuller and I saw everything through your eyes, which taught me even more ways to heal and help others. When you married and then gave birth to your daughter, I thought my heart would burst again because she was like us from the moment she appeared in the world. We are a rare breed of women, and for that I am thankful. Thank you for coming to me, daughter."

As mother and daughter stared lovingly at each other, the door burst open.

"You thought you could leave without me, grandmother?" Lidija, confident, beautiful and in her youthful radiance, entered the room. She walked to the other side of the bed and grasped her other hand. Both girls were holding her hands now. "I love you to the moon and the stars. You are forever in my heart, forever guiding me and my healing skills. Thank you for all that you are and all that you have done."

Lidija hugged her grandmother tightly before sitting next to her on the bed. "Do you need anything? Tea, water, food?"

"No, my darling. I do not need anything but I am so grateful for you and your mother to be here next to me as I journey to the other side. I love you so much, granddaughter. Stay true to your heart. And I love you, my daughter. I will always guide and protect you both from the other side. It will not be long now."

They stayed in silence, holding hands for a few hours that led into the early morning, when the silence on this earth is the loudest and most profound.

The healer felt into her body then, and could sense her heart slowing down and becoming weaker. She smiled at both of them and squeezed their hands one last time before she exhaled her final breath.

Love and peace were her final thoughts as she left her earthly body.

***

A few lessons learned in this lifetime:

Yes, you can have a fulfilled loving life with family with an absent romantic life. However, despite all of the love you feel towards children and grandchildren, resentment can grow towards men (dead husband) which can lead to turning off emotions towards men altogether. This leads to an unbalanced soul loop of alternating between searching for unconditional love (in all the wrong places) and running away from it/denying it truly exists. Never experiencing love with your soulmate can lead to an unsatisfied life.

Chapter 9

The Glory of Rome!

❖

203 BC

The Roman Republic was in its heyday. Senators were in power and the war machine was in full swing. The fight for power and wealth was constant, and the need to outwit fellow Senators to gain more was only matched by the hedonism taking place in their villas. Senate assemblies were held in places dedicated to the gods, where filibusters could last for an entire day, and they could veto a dictator or magistrate's rulings.

This event was not as he had expected.

After running around the Forum all day going from house to house, trying to finalize the agreement amongst the majority of the senators, Marco had decided that he would treat himself to the party that his rival senator Cassius was throwing.

Walking into the party, he was quite surprised.

Here the entirety of the senate and their wives, lovers and mistresses as well as manservants and female slaves, all finely adorned and perfumed were walking around half clothed or completely naked.

It seemed to be an entirely different party than he thought it would be. Marco had assumed there would be dinner and drunkenness as well as arguments over politics, but this seemed to be an unusually refined affair of the highest extravagance.

Cassius had spared no expense.

As Marco glanced around the large, high-ceilinged room filled with cushions and couches, brightly burning candles, an over-abundance of food, flowing wine, tittering laughter, and the sound of bare feet on marble as people walked to and fro, he looked for familiar faces.

Glancing through the many colorfully decorated rooms, he took in the statues and tapestries on the wall. There were images of gladiatorial games, horse races, and busts of Epictetus and Marcus Aurelius, among others.

Upon closer review, he realized there were many nude slaves mingling throughout the party as well. He always thought it was cruel to let a slave experience the delight of delicious food and abundant drink and fleshly pleasures before going back to their mundane, sad existence in servitude.

But, Marco was not the host and that was Cassius' error in judgement. It provided an opportunity for the slaves to think about their situation and rise up in rebellion every once in a while.

If he had to witness another riot in the streets from the peasants after this party, he would take off for his villa near the ocean for a month or so. He hated to see them beaten to death by the military. The blood and gore was not something he enjoyed.

He much preferred luxury and art to the warring and brutish military scenes. Personally, he had a distaste for bloodshed. But he was, after all, Roman.

~~~

Marco had never married for the sake of his career – how could he divide his attention between a career and possibly falling in love with his wife or their subsequent children?

He had too much work to do and not enough spare time. Also, there was too much corruption as well as countless unsolved poisonings and accidental deaths, even amidst the Senators' wives and mistresses. He was glad that he had never married.

Clearing his thoughts from these meanderings, he ambled into another room.

Waved over by a friend of his, he joined a group of four senators, smiles all around as each of them were enjoying the show.

"It is too early for me to get into the spirit of this party," one senator said.

"I will need to keep quaffing the wine as quickly as possible. Then I will not mind if my wife watches me with anyone of my choosing," another said.

"Your wife is enjoying herself in the next room. I saw her just before I came in here and joined you!" the third senator replied.

They all started laughing.

"Thank the gods!" the married senator exclaimed as he downed a goblet of wine and headed towards a dark-haired slave girl.

All slaves were required to wear a large coarse copper bracelet so that they could be easily identified in all situations. These copper bracelets were given to them by their masters. The free people were identified by small silver bracelets. The wealthier class either wore gold or nothing at all, depending on the occasion and the host.

The bracelets were another way to subjugate the masses; dominate them by marking them for easy identification, especially in a group setting.

"Marco, I wanted to congratulate you on your agreement this afternoon. I know you worked hard to get it signed by almost all of the senators. It will pass now," his friend praised, slapping him on the back cheerfully.

"I had little faith you would get the majority to sign it. Very clever to add that small part at the end about the Senators getting a stipend after serving for fifteen years in the Senate. You might yet become a master politician!" said Albus, a senior senator.

"I appreciate your praise, Albus. After all, you will be the first to get the stipend," Marco rejoined with a smirk at the elder man.

Albus hooted and slapped his thigh. "Always quick with the truth, young man. Be careful who you speak too boisterously about the truth to around here. There are those in the Senate who spend most of their days hiding it as one buries precious gold and jewels on their country estate to keep out of the hands of thieves and government. Or their own wives!"

They all laughed.

There was no use denying what Albus warned of.

Of all of the Senators, Albus was one of the few remaining long-standing ones left breathing. Once they had outlived their usefulness or sanity, they were removed from office by younger men who coveted their position. The political intrigue was deadly; deadly in a way that was proclaimed to be a 'natural death' by 'dying in their sleep' or 'falling off of a horse' or by a 'heart attack'.

The masses believed the stories while the Senators played their games and plotted their next moves with the ever burning question: Who would have and yield the most power?

As the four senators in the group all nodded their heads in agreement, Marco knew it was time to move to another room.

"Excuse me gentlemen, I must relieve myself before the real festivities begin after everyone is quite intoxicated." Bowing, he left them and meandered into the adjoining room.

~~~

He spotted a very familiar face. Although Marco had not invited his on-again, off-again mistress here with him, he saw her with her trader husband, enjoying a lovemaking scene between two men and one woman.

A woman walked by him and lightly touched him on the arm. "I trust you are enjoying yourself, Senator Marco," she breathed out of her luscious, pomegranate-colored lips.

Restraining himself from jumping at her touch, he smiled. It was Cassius' wife Drusilla; his enemy's wife.

"Very much so. It is a lovely party," he laughed as two beautiful naked women walked by in front of them.

"Good. I do not want you to leave early as you normally leave parties. Stay a while and see who takes your fancy. There could be a woman or two who would love your effortless charm and banter," Drusilla returned as she looked up at him coyly.

"Perhaps you could tell me who these women might be so that I might avoid the rest," he responded.

Running her hand along the low cut cloth that exposed most of her breasts, he realized Drusilla was talking about herself. That would be very bad to act upon, considering his rivalry with her husband.

Yet, it was like dangling fresh meat in front of a starving tiger.

"My lady, that would be most disastrous for the both of us, bearing in mind that your husband hates me."

"I did not take you for a coward, Marco, no matter what my husband says about you," she countered.

Marco knew that she was trying to provoke him and he decided that he needed to put distance between them or he could end up poisoned by Cassius.

"I appreciate your hospitality, and I will think upon your suggestion, Drusilla. Enjoy your party," he responded as he nodded to her and walked away.

His thoughts blurred as he searched for a safe spot to observe the party from. The last thing he needed right now was the fury of her husband, although it was common knowledge that her husband loved his mistresses and paraded them around town unabashedly.

Drusilla was gorgeous and fair-haired, which was rare amongst the darker-skinned Romans. Her beauty was spoken of and envied amongst the other senators who took wives based on political or monetary gain, not necessarily for looks. She had been kept from life in Rome by her father, a proud senator named Septimus, in order to keep her away from the evils of the city and the pressure to marry her off for mere advantages.

Septimus had been incredibly proud and protective of her beauty that she finally snuck away from the villa at the age of seventeen to come to Rome unhindered by Septimus' watchful eye. It had been on this disastrous occasion that Cassius had found Drusilla, seduced her and then demanded to marry her within two days.

All before anyone else in Rome could even see her.

Once he had her firmly ensnared, Cassius paraded her around town like a prized horse, and she quickly began to regret her decision.

Her once proud father died shortly after their marriage, his heart broken by giving his daughter away to such a dreadfully selfish and horrible man.

Drusilla, in return, had blamed her husband entirely and declared she would never give Cassius an heir. She refused to pass on his bloodline.

Prudently, she had professed this in private to her most trusted maid. She was not naïve enough to say this to her husband's face because Cassius would kill her or have her killed. He must believe that she would give him an heir.

The only reason Marco knew any of this was that he had taken her maid as one of his mistresses for a few years in order to learn the inner-workings of his detested rival's household.

Stumbling upon this treasure trove was one of the greatest pieces of information he could ever obtain, and yet one he could never use.

He would not put Drusilla at risk, for he had loved her father. Septimus had been his mentor and had taken Marco under his tutelage when he had first come to the Senate many years ago.

'And it all becomes one big circle, doesn't it - this Colosseum of life?' Marco thought to himself.

~~~

In reality, the Roman military mechanism had created an amazing mass of slaves. The normal people that thought they voted for the Senate did not realize that they had no control over the outcome and only the illusion of choice whereas the military kept law and order while expanding the slavery into other lands. All for "The Glory of Rome!"

That's how the Republic grew larger and larger, richer and richer, even as they continued exploiting and controlling the people by means of the military.

And they were at the 'top', these senators. Rome was at its peak; it was unparalleled in strength, knowledge and lands.

At least that's how they were writing the history that men would find in hundreds of years and say "Oh glory be, what an amazing society!" History is rewritten by the victors.

In fact, the agreement that Marco had been running around getting signed by the other senators today had been about denying the low level military slaves any monies until they had reached a ten year career point. Then they would be paid a monthly stipend that depended upon their service to Rome.

If they remained in military service after the ten years, they would have a retirement of sorts paid for by Rome. If not, they would be killed 'in the line of duty' with their families none the wiser.

More soldiers would be 'recruited' as the military took more land and spread the patriotic news throughout the Republic. There really was no choice for poor people who had too many children or people in the lands the Republic conquered; the boys would be enticed to march off to war with the promise of payment once they returned or they were slaves that were forced or sold into it.

Usually, the soldiers never returned home because war was endless and there was always a new land to send them to "civilize" in the name of the Republic.

This was a win-win for the senators. Less money going out and more slaves for the army. Everyone got to be a patriot and cheer on the greatest empire the world had ever seen!

Yet even he could see the writing on the wall. Eventually, this system would fail. There was no possibility that it could survive another hundred or so years at this hectic pace. The rate of mortality and rebellion was rising although the Senate lied to the masses about the numbers.

The people believed the most commonly heard lies; so it was easy to spread falsehoods to keep the masses from discovering how much power they actually would have if they rose up against the chosen few.

There was not enough military in the city itself to hold back all of its citizens if they decided to take over.

~~~

Grabbing a goblet of wine from a table, he drank deeply, relishing the feel of its liquid warmth heating his belly.

He was beckoned by the two naked women he had seen earlier whilst speaking with Drusilla. They were clearly tipsy and having a fantastic time. Perfect!

"Hello, ladies. Do you need more wine?" he asked them.

They giggled. The slightly taller one said, "No, kind sir, we are happy as we are. Would you like to explore with us?"

"Explore with you?"

"Yes, we would like to see the rest of this villa," the shorter one answered while running a finger down his chest.

"As you wish, ladies. Lead the way!"

They each grabbed one of his arms and swiftly led him into the back of the home where a large staircase was surrounded by plants and large handcrafted, valuable pottery. Each of them seized a goblet of wine from a nearby table and smiled at him.

Leading him up the stairs, they veered left towards the first room in the hall. Upon entering, he noticed they were in a room full of cushions, flowers and incense burning along with candles scattered throughout the draperies.

The room reminded him of a drawing he had seen of a similar room in the palace of a desert king, a king of the Arabs – full of colorful cushions, drapes and glass lamps, designed for comfort and relaxation.

Closing the door behind him, the taller one said, "We need to remove your robe, Senator. You look stifled from having so many clothes on."

The shorter one grinned up at him as she started to undress him. She was quite lovely with dark eyes and long dark hair that looked black in this lighting. Her teeth were even and white which meant she was of a high class and breeding.

Marco had noticed earlier that neither of them wore a bracelet. He did not know either of them or where they came from, what household they were from. But it was not important, for they would not be at the party unless they were invited and known by Cassius.

"Could I know your names or what you would prefer to be called? Or should I call you beautiful woman one and beautiful woman two?"

Smiling, the taller one replied, "I am Rossa and this is Maria."

"Rossa, for the red hair?"

"No, after my mother," the taller one answered.

"Well both of your mothers must have been beauties," Marco retorted.

"Ah, we heard you were a charmer, but now we know you truly are," Maria commented.

"Oh, I feel that I am at a disadvantage. I know nothing of either of you. Are you married? Will your husbands barge in here in the middle of this and murder me? Or your fathers?"

They both laughed in unison. Their laughs were equally provocative and seductive, and smooth like honey.

Being a suspicious man, he glanced quickly around the room to ensure nobody was hiding in the drapes to kill him. But these two women could poison him as well. Marco did not doubt the hate Cassius had for him.

He started to pull his robes back on. He would not fall for a noticeable trap such as this; it would take more cleverness to kill him than two beautiful women!

Rossa and Maria looked at each other with surprise and then shrugged.

"You do not want to be with us?" Rossa asked him.

"Ladies, you are both very lovely but I have overstayed my welcome," Marco replied as he walked towards the door. "I have business to attend to this evening. Thank you for the tour and your presence."

He bowed respectfully to them and scurried out of the door. Closing it behind him, he almost yelped as he ran right into Drusilla.

"I wondered where you had run off to," she purred.

Her eyes were a bit glazed as if she had partaken of a few more drinks than she normally would have.

Handing him her goblet, she commanded, "Drink up. You look uneasy."

As he drank, Marco watched her closely, unsure of her game. Was Cassius using her as a standby if the other two women could not murder him? His murder would be very easy to cover up at an excessive gathering such as this.

Heavily sighing, Drusilla beckoned for Marco to follow her. "I would like to show you something," she whispered as she flowed past him into the corridor.

Raising his left eyebrow in response, he trailed her. He only hoped she wasn't walking him into a death trap. Marco wanted to trust her out of his love for her late father.

Taking a key from her belt, she unlocked a door quietly. They walked into a well-lit room full of art, sculptures, parchments and bound parchments, rolled up maps, and tools of unique and foreign designs.

"What's all of this?" he asked as he took in the length of the room. It was filled to the brim and double the size of the room he had just been in.

She smiled slyly, similar to a cat that caught a canary. "This, dear Marco, is everything that I inherited from my father that Cassius did not sell before I knew what he was doing. I would like to give you something from this room. My father would have wanted that."

He was speechless.

He never dreamed in his entire life that he would get to pick out something that belonged to Septimus, his beloved mentor! Without Septimus, he would not be as far in the Senate as he was today.

Walking in a circle, Marco pointed to everything and exclaimed, "Anything out of this that I want?"

"Yes!" she answered excitedly. "I would never be able to get through half of what is in here and I know that you will cherish the item that you pick out. Please, take your time. I will give you the key and return downstairs to the party. Discreetly give me the key back once you are finished. There are spies everywhere."

Handing him the key, she murmured over her shoulder as she headed to the door, "Marco, please lock the door behind me. Cassius would love the opportunity to barge into this room and burn it all. It is best that he does not know you are in here."

With his heart pounding with anticipation while thoughts of what Cassius would do to him if they were found out, what he would do to

Drusilla, Marco replied, "Of course! Thank you so much for this amazing gift! I do not know how I can ever repay you for it."

"I'm sure we can think of something," she responded as she winked at him.

Then she was gone.

Marco quickly locked the door behind her, unwilling to allow any intrusions while he searched for the only thing he knew he wanted; the leather bound journal that Septimus wrote in daily. He had seen it upon his desk once and knew Septimus kept it locked away in a hidden place. It contained many of his teachings to Marco, along with other ideas that Septimus had not had time to explain before his death.

Again, he thought, this party was turning into an unexpected surprise!

As he searched through the parchments, wooden crates and table tops, Marco's mind wandered. He had wondered if, and partially hoped that, she was bringing him into this room to seduce him.

Drusilla was a beautiful woman but also the daughter of Septimus. At one point many years ago, Marco had felt that Septimus was going to introduce he and Drusilla. That Septimus wanted them to be married.

Marco would have loved her and treated her well as his wife, Septimus would still be alive, and Marco's career would be much further along, he believed.

However, there was no use of thinking of what might have been; he only envisioned the future now, and how to make the best of it, as her father had taught him.

Septimus had been a big proponent of mind mastery and using it to bring fortune, health and Senate leadership.

"It is good to see all possible angles of a situation, yet even better if you can reimagine the scene going exactly how you wish it to go, and feeling that jubilation from having your wish granted. That is what makes the master, instead of the slave to the negative or 'realistic' scenarios," he would say to Marco every day.

Until Marco had started to say it back and think it in his head. And that is how most of Marco's documents and legislations got signed in the Senate to this day; by this one little thinking habit that had served him well.

Shuffling some of the art work around, he stumbled upon a medium sized chest. It was locked.

"Where would Septimus keep the key?" he pondered out loud as he glanced around.

In the back of the room, he spotted a small desk with smaller sculptures on it. Large sculptures concealed it from the front of the room so that a person would be unable to see it if they were at the doorway.

He slowly and carefully made his way to the desk. Marco knew Septimus; there would be a hidden compartment.

Running his hands along every inch of the desk, his right hand found the tiny latch on the side panel next to a small drawer. Pressing the latch with one finger while holding onto the bottom of the drawer with his other hand, a hidden compartment sprung out and almost smacked him in the face.

He chuckled.

Septimus was a cunning man; if Marco had been inept, the concealed drawer would have hit him and left a mark or knocked him out. Either way, the culprit that opened the drawer would be easily identifiable.

Picking up the key, he walked back over to the chest and knelt down to unlock it. Lifting the lid of the chest, he saw that it was filled with pieces of cloth, jewels and feathers.

"Interesting," Marco murmured as he thrust his hands inside the chest to rummage through the contents.

At the bottom left of the chest, he felt the smoothness of leather. Pulling out the item, he knew this was the journal.

Smiling hugely, he tucked the journal into his robe and shut the lid of the chest. Locking it, he returned the key back to the secret compartment and closed it.

Shuffling some art work around and making it look as though Marco would not have seen the desk or the chest, he scanned the room for something else to take with him.

He did not want Cassius or Drusilla to know about the journal concealed within his robe.

He grabbed a nearby item that meant nothing to him and proceeded to exit the room.

After locking the door behind him, he stood by it for a few minutes, ensuring nobody was watching him and also to calm his racing heart.

~~~

"I didn't know you were still here," Rossa said to him softly as he sauntered down the corridor in deep thought.

Marco almost flew out of his skin.

He had been so absorbed in the journal hidden in his robe, the rolled map he now carried in his hand and how he was going to return the key to Drusilla, that he had not noticed Rossa and Maria exiting the candlelit room they had all been in earlier.

"Oh, hello! I was slightly detained," he professed happily to them as he held up the map.

They both glanced behind him and seeing nobody, Maria stated, "Since you are here now, we should all go downstairs and have another drink!"

He laughed and agreed, "Yes, let's all go enjoy ourselves."

They each grabbed one of his elbows and led him swiftly away from the candlelit room and down the stairs.

~~~

Two hours later, Marco was ready to leave in earnest.

He had carried this map around with him the entire night and witnessed hedonistic scenes that he would not be able to un-see. He had left Maria and Rossa in one of the other rooms so that he could find Drusilla and get out of this villa.

All that he had to do now was get the key back to Drusilla undetected by her husband's spies.

'Easy,' he thought sarcastically. The entire villa was filled with people.

However, an idea sprang into his head.

Walking casually over to one of the many refreshment tables, he held the key in his hand where it was hidden by the large rolled up map. Confirming that nobody was at the table or close to him, Marco glanced about the room as he stood next to the table. Tucking the map gently under his arm, he deftly and noiselessly dropped the key into one of the wine goblets.

He crouched and picked up the goblet with the key in it and the one next to it while keeping the map positioned under his arm.

Noticing that Drusilla was on the other side of the room, he made his way over to her slowly.

She smiled at him and said, "I hope you have had a wonderful time. It seems you have stayed later than you normally would."

He handed her the glass and admitted the truth. "I have had the most wonderful evening." Dropping his voice to a whisper, he murmured, "I loved your father very much. Thank you for allowing this evening."

Tipping the wine goblet, her eyes widened slightly as the key hit her mouth.

She smiled at him and replied, "You are welcome. You must excuse me; I need to see to something. Have a lovely rest of your evening, Marco."

He watched her walk away, sat his glass down and then turned to leave as well.

His arm not holding the map was suddenly gripped by Cassius.

"And what do you have there, Marco? Another legislation to sign? It seems a bit too large for that," Cassius snarled at him.

"No, it's just a map. I'm going to see if it has any value or if it's simply a decoration," Marco answered, showing his exasperation as he removed Cassius' hand from his arm.

"Why would you bring the map to my party?"

"In fact, I picked it up here from a friend that had asked me to determine the map's value," Marco lied.

Cassius glared at him, unsure if he was lying or not. Senators were very adept at not telling the truth while keeping a straight face.

Smirking at Cassius, Marco said, "I've got work to do, Cassius. If you will excuse me, I will see you when the Senate convenes next."

Nodding, Cassius responded, "I am watching you, Marco. You are up to something. I will see you soon."

That sounded more like a threat than anything else, Marco gathered.

Turning on his heel, Marco left his rival looking after him while he left the debauched party as rapidly as he could.

~~~

He rose early the next morning and excitedly started reading the journal.

Marco needed the small mental break this journal provided since he had been working like a mule in order for his most recent legislation to pass. Trying to make Rome less corrupt and friendlier towards foreigners would be the death of me, he surmised.

He hoped to leave a legacy of peace and goodwill instead of constant war and greed. They needed more unity and love, less corruption, infighting and conquering new territories. Rome was spread too thin right now and it needed to remember its own people.

It was time to start looking inward and making the country itself into a powerhouse, not just scattered cities and towns that had a certain use or natural resources to be exploited.

However, today Marco was going to take the day off.

He would go to the market after he read a bit of Septimus' journal. He enjoyed seeing the market alive and bustling and had not done that in many months.

Septimus wrote similar to his speaking style, eloquently and witty with a dash of absurdity thrown in. Marco chuckled at some of his descriptions from the beginning pages. This journal was from the last two years of Septimus' life yet, as Marco progressed further into it, it was painful for him to read.

Septimus was highly esteemed by Marco and many people in the Senate. He had been known as a fair and honorable man with a perpetually optimistic outlook; however, in this journal his feelings of despair regarding Drusilla's marriage broke Marco's heart.

Selfishly, Marco had desired the journal in order to learn more wisdom from his mentor. Instead, he was shedding tears of sorrow for the anguish that Septimus did not even reveal to his mentee at the time.

Marco put the journal down. It was too much for him at the moment. He decided it was time to hide it in his locked chest hidden under his floor and head to the market.

He would take the map to a merchant in the marketplace. He might as well pretend he cared about the map just in case Cassius' spies were following him.

The last thing he wanted was to give Cassius any reason to destroy anything in Drusilla's room full of items from her father. Or to give him any reason to think that Marco had an item from that room.

Marco would die before he would let Cassius get his hands on the journal. Cassius thrived off of the pain of others; he had even laughed when he was told of Septimus' death during a Senate meeting!

Shaking his head, Marco stared into the marketplace. He didn't even realize he had already arrived until he almost bumped into a merchant's stall.

Typically, he was not a man that let his feelings distract him from his political purpose. However, Marco reasoned, it was not a normal day when a man truly comprehends the deep heartbreak of his mentor, written in Septimus' own handwriting, which then led to his mentor's premature demise.

Marco needed a drink.

Glancing around the marketplace, he saw an outdoor café with the proprietor pouring drinks.

Ambling towards it with his purposeful gait, Marco sat down. The proprietor came over immediately, understanding that Marco was a high paying patron due to his dress and gold bracelet.

"Wine, please," Marco ordered.

Running inside, the proprietor came back swiftly with his best goblet and his finest wine. Pouring him a glass, the proprietor nodded as Marco threw down a coin.

"Keep them coming."

"Yes, sir," the proprietor agreed as he snatched the coin up and marched off to pour the cheaper wine to his other customers.

"Here's to you, Septimus. I am sorry I was not there for you as a friend. I miss you and your lessons every day," Marco saluted the dead senator, raised his goblet, and took a large mouthful of wine.

Swallowing it down, he grimaced.

It was not the best wine but it was not the worst he had ever had. It would do for an impromptu mid-day memorial. He never acted so carelessly during the day because of his ambition, and he had never toasted Septimus or his passing.

It was high time that he did so, Marco mused. But truthfully, he wanted to forget the sadness from the pages he had read.

He would get to the map merchant later.

~~~

As the sun was getting closer to sunset, Marco decided it was time he should visit the map merchant and then head home. He would go to sleep early and wake up with the sun in order to finish the work he had put off today.

Turning to leave after paying the proprietor, he noticed that Rossa and Maria were in a silk seller's stall across the marketplace. He grinned and jauntily made his way over to them.

"Ladies, you are both looking very exquisite on this fine day," he said charmingly.

He could smell both of them as he stood within arm's reach.

They smiled up at him and then started to giggle.

"What are you both laughing about?" he asked them.

Rossa replied, "We are laughing because our husbands are lovers, which you might already know, and they both think that after they disappeared at the party together last night that we spent the entire evening with you, Marco. But we all know that this is not the case."

"We did have a lovely time together but I was preoccupied regarding this map," he held the map out with one arm towards them. "In truth, I'm on my way to the map merchant currently to see the value of this for my friend."

Marco decided in that moment that the map lie would continue expanding. 'Why not,' he thought to himself. 'Cassius' spies would have this added confirmation. Oh, the games we play in order to be powerful senators...'

The ladies nodded and Rossa said, "Yes. Our husbands can be strange at times. Especially when they believe they have been wronged or outwitted."

"Why are you telling me this?" Marco boldly questioned them both.

Maria answered, "They are around here at the market and we wanted you to know in case you ran into them. My husband loves to pretend he is jealous of any man that I might look at."

"They tell us we are not to lay with any man in case we might get pregnant but then they are always together and not sleeping with us. Last night at the party after you left the room, we were with someone else," added Rossa.

'Why would they tell me all of this?' he pondered to himself.

"Should I be worried that they are going to try to harm me?" Marco prodded. "Who are your husbands? Do I know them?"

"No, you don't know them. They are very wealthy traders that think they can buy their way into the good graces of senators and nobles," Rossa responded as Maria shook her head.

"And did you correct their suspicions of me being in that room with you two last night?" he asked as the hairs on the back of his neck stood up.

He had a funny feeling about this.

Maria smiled and said, "No, we did not. Our husbands are harmless and will do nothing to you. They do not wish their affair to be exposed as it might hurt their business or so they think…"

"But we would also like to keep the other man's identity a secret from them because he deals with our husbands quite often. They have contracts that might suffer and vice versa," interjected Rossa.

"And what happens when they find out that I was not the one you spent the night with? Because I cannot guarantee that my friend will not be happily telling everyone about the map and why I have it. Then your husbands will find out that you both have fibbed," Marco countered.

He was not going to take the blame for something that he had no part of. He already had Cassius to worry about; he didn't need another enemy.

As the three of them continued discussing this ridiculous lie about last night's party, an event that he was now coming to regret he even attended, Marco did not hear the odd high-pitched scream coming from a man in another stall.

The man came racing towards Marco's turned back with a dagger held out in front of him and plunged it into Marco's right side.

Looking up as he grabbed his side to stop the blood, Marco saw a strong, broad-shouldered man with a twisted grin on his face, sneering at him pitilessly as he stabbed Marco in the abdomen in a move that looked like he was embracing Marco, and whispered into Marco's ear, "I know what you did! You will never touch my wife again!"

"What…" was all Marco could say as the man shoved Marco away from him.

Maria and Rossa stood embracing each other in shock as Marco fell to his knees on the stones of the marketplace.

The market had gone quiet as Marco's wounds soaked the stones red with his blood.

Someone shouted, "Murder! Get the soldiers!"

There were at least a dozen witnesses standing in a circle around him but a few had run off to find soldiers.

Marco tried to stay upright but he felt so weak, so drained of energy; he was becoming lightheaded.

'He could outlive this attack, right? The wounds were hopefully not that deep,' he wistfully believed. 'If he could just remain upright, on his knees, he would make it.'

He was not ready to die yet. There were so many political moves he had yet to make, so many ideas for new legislations that he wanted to get passed. He wanted to leave a true legacy.

He wanted to see Drusilla and tell her about the journal, that he had it.

He needed more time.

"I can't die now. Not yet," he murmured as his strength gave way and he fell unceremoniously to the ground.

His attacker stood there, chuckling as he stared at Marco lying on his back with blood leaking everywhere. A man stood behind the attacker, his eyes still widened in horror and disbelief.

Rossa dropped to her knees beside Marco and placed her hand on his arm. "Please, don't die," she whispered with tears running down her cheeks.

He smiled at her in an attempt to be chivalrous despite the dire situation; she knew it was partly her fault that he had been stabbed.

Soldiers approached heavily and Maria pointed at her own husband who happened to be the attacker. The other onlookers pointed at him as well.

The crazed man looked appalled as the soldiers seized him by the arms and hauled him away, with two men trailing after the guards reciting their witnessed accounts. The shocked man, Rossa's husband, had tears in his eyes as he watched his lover being dragged away.

Maria sat on Marco's other side and gently laid her hand against his cheek as he felt his heart beating slower and slower. Marco tried to give her a smile but it was too hard.

His eyes were losing focus and he looked up at the sky. A few birds flew by and he felt a great calm settle over him.

He closed his eyes. Everything was beautiful. Everything was warm. The golden light was enveloping him now. There was nothing more to think about or worry about.

He could no longer feel his body or the pain or the loving hands that lay upon his dying form.

His last breath sputtered out of his body as the two women sat soundlessly by his side with tears streaming down their faces.

A few lessons learned in this lifetime:

When you live a life only for legacy and political gain, you die alone and learn in the end that your life was empty and futile. Dying with regrets because you did not marry/try to love someone, and only focused on your career, leaves your soul in a love loop. A good career does not equate to the love of another soul.

Chapter 10

Versailles

❖

1692 CE

The Sun King, Louis XIV, had moved the royal French Court to the Palace of Versailles in 1682. Spectacular parties, parlor games, the finest plays of the period, hunting and much more were common activities at the Palace. Protestants had been forced to convert or leave the country in 1685, trade was booming, and Louis was winning strategic military campaigns with the help of his innovative Superintendent, who also oversaw the building of aqueducts and engineering improvements to the City of Versailles, the Palace and more. Louis' reign, until his death in 1715, is known as "Le Grand Siècle" (The Great Century).

It was through no fault of her own that this accursed place, and even her own life reflected within these walls, was a foolish spectacle.

She had tried her hardest to be loved and respected, and to stay above the gossip and hurtful prattle the court tended to sink into.

Always dressed differently, elegantly and in her own style, she tended to recycle an almost angelic presence despite the color of her dresses or the newest fashion of the year.

How many years had she been here, Gabrielle pondered?

The years all bled into each other and one was much the same as the next.

Endless parties that continued to be marvelous fun with games, drink and food, and usually followed by an all-night miniature gathering in someone's chambers that bordered on sinfully extreme and hedonistic revelry.

She chose to avoid most of the latter, unless exotic persons or foreign royalty were in attendance such as fortune tellers, Arabic musicians or African Kings. Instead, she would head to the lake or one of the fountains, as they were quiet, while everyone else partied or slept.

There was no other place she loved more than the lake. It was not truly a lake but that is what she called it since it was rather large to be a pond. It reminded her of the small lake on the property she had grown up on; the lands she had been unable to go back to due to the King.

He would not let any of them leave Versailles.

It was a shame really. She had missed being with her father on his deathbed and his burial. Once her father's health had rapidly declined within his rooms at Court, the King bade him return to his home in order to not infect the other inhabitants of Versailles.

Her father happily accepted his departure yet was distraught that the King had denied his daughter accompanying him home. She felt that this aided her father's rapid deterioration, for he did not live past three weeks upon his arrival home.

As the only heir of the entire family, she had received the totality of the estate due to a lack of male cousins, uncles, or bastard male children. Regardless of this massive weight that now fell on her shoulders, the King had denied her passage to take care of the family business; demanding her land custodian and estate supervisor come to her, as if they had naught else to do but journey for two days to get here and give her an in-person report.

Huffing out her breath in a mix of exasperation and acquiescence, she knew why the King had kept her here.

Sitting on all of the land, inheritance and rental dues that she had received from her father's passing meant that she was a very wealthy heiress and must be married off quickly.

King Louis wanted it to be a very valuable alliance as he counted on her unwavering obedience and rational mind.

Although he was older now, the King still loved a good party and pretending to be a good matchmaker, albeit for his own personal gain. He would claim it was for the "Good of France" but in the end, every alliance or marriage was for loyalty, land gains or money in his coffers.

Thank God she was not beautiful, or King Louis might have tried to make her his mistress before he married her off. Although his taking of mistresses was an error of judgment from his youth, it was still whispered that he would have whomever he wanted despite his age, declaration of subservience to God's laws, and matured wisdom.

But, none of this was a concern for her.

Gabrielle could not even pass as pretty, with a nose designed for an ugly, large man and a bushy set of black eyebrows; both of which were compliments of her father. Her mother had been a beauty in her youth, and apparently had weak genes, because her daughter had inherited nothing from her in the looks department.

Her prettiest feature was her slightly plump and rose colored mouth. It was a kissable mouth. Her maid told her so whenever she was feeling down about her lack of lovers or even the prospect of one. Gabrielle's eyes were almost black and gave her a look of "Death" wearing a black cloak when he came to claim the sick and dying, or so she imagined.

At least her body was pleasant enough with curves in the right places and a thin stomach and legs. Her hair was also agreeable since it was long, black, and lustrous. Supposedly, it was the envy of a few ladies at court.

Growing up in her father's large estate, she had never felt ugly or alone. Here in this place bursting with conceit, greed and plotting, she knew she was ugly and alone. That was made quite evident to her by all of the men and women in this massive, opulent building.

The King was the only person who ever invited her to a private party. He would make her sit next to every new arrival at court and accompany them on a tour around the grounds. This was his way, and she always obeyed his suggestions and commands.

However, her body and mind yearned for more. She was almost twenty-one now. There was no time to play around any longer; she should have been married years ago.

If he did not marry Gabrielle off soon, she could be doomed to a solitary spinster life! And the King was no spring chicken either. Once he died, she would be banished to her estate by his heir, she was sure. She would banish her own self if the roles were reversed.

It truly was a horrible lot, to be born an ugly woman. Worse, she could have been born a servant, she conjectured.

A servant could at least enjoy sex with whomever they wished, though. No matter how ugly they were, there was always someone to have sex with.

As a wealthy, titled woman now, she was destined to only have sex with whoever her husband would be.

This court was so overrun with sex and mistresses despite a few priests being consistently present. The King had declared years ago that they were all to attend Church services with a minimum attendance to mass each week being required.

Thus, she had taken it upon herself to be the epitome of decorum and King Louis enjoyed her submission to, and respect of, his directives.

But alas, here they all were, filling their bellies full of wine at supper and breaking dishes while a few rowdier people started to climb up on top of tables to deliver some form of entertainment.

The King had left an hour ago claiming to need sleep on this lively Thursday evening.

Therefore, Gabrielle would wait another few hours before heading out to her quiet spot by the lake. Perhaps, as it was warm despite the sun going down, she would row a little boat out onto it.

Sometimes she preferred this to her bed and would fall asleep in the boat, lulled by the sway caused by the wind, only to be awakened with the sunrise or by her maid yelling for her from the shore when she had found her missing from her bed.

It could be a rather lonely world when a person's only friend was their maid, she contemplated, in the midst of a roaring event that made her feel even more isolated.

~~~

The louder the evening's festivities became, the quicker she could escape to the lake. Her continuous praying for the noise to increase seemed to be working.

She pretended to observe everything that was happening so that she would be reported as being attentive; most likely taking notes in her head, they would say to the King's spies. Everyone was spying on everyone else for gain and the King's favor.

But Gabrielle did not care anymore. The strain of this constrictive life was beyond anything she wished for. She wanted her quiet life at home; the one she had grown up with.

Even if she married, King Louis would make her stay with her new husband in Versailles. They would not even be allowed to leave for a honeymoon or to visit her lands, and who knew if the King's son would continue this stifling tradition once he ascended to the throne. Most likely he would.

The thought made her stomach turn sour. Gingerly sitting down her wine glass, she surveyed the room again.

Spotting all the single, marriageable men spread throughout the massive candle lit room, her stomach started to roil at the prospect of marrying any of them.

There was not one genuinely respectable man amongst them. They had all been twisted by this place, if they weren't already by the time they had arrived at Versailles.

Similar to what the isolation of prison did to men, this structure of distortion and perversion allowed for no escape. This was unquestionably a prison masquerading as a lavish party.

And the only way to get out was death.

"Well, that is that," she softly murmured to herself.

Her appetite and mood were completely crippled by her thoughts at this juncture and she decided that it was time to head for fresh air. Perhaps that would cheer her up and give her happy thoughts.

With slightly renewed hope, she stood up and started to head for the nearest door when her arm was seized by a man she vaguely recognized.

"Mademoiselle, I have heard a rumor that we are to be betrothed," he spoke into her ear as the party noises had increased in the room behind them.

She inhaled sharply and took a step back because she had suddenly put a name to the face.

This was beyond incredible, she thought. The King would not dare to marry her off to him!

This man's father was recently arrested and guillotined due to his refusal to turn on his Protestant faith and become Catholic, keeping with his family line of scientists and scholarly beliefs. His integrity had gotten him killed.

"Impossible," Gabrielle replied as she gracefully used her left hand to remove his tight grip from her arm.

"I think improbable is the word you are searching for because nothing at this court is impossible. But yes, according to my uncle's information, King Louis is currently negotiating your marriage contract to yours truly." He pointed a finger to himself while giving her a radiant and charming smile.

Upon finishing his attempt at flirting, he had the impudence to bow to her like a knight of old who had saved a helpless maiden in a tower.

"That would be a disaster," she replied truthfully while sizing him up with one eyebrow cocked.

She had never taken the time to look at him because she had assumed the King would kill him shortly and give all of his lands away to a more loyal, Catholic subject after his father's death.

"A disaster for you, yes, most likely. But it would be a great feat for me and mine, as I'm sure you're aware. My family is in a quandary since my father's disavowment to pay the taxes and give faithfully to the Church. It will take many years before his rejection is forgotten by society and the King. These are important times," he said sorrowfully with a frown and serious expression in his eyes.

She shook her head from side to side. Really, what game was the King playing at here? She would be able to figure out the angle if she was sitting in silence. The party noise was deafening.

He stared at her while she tried to control her face. If she were aligned with him that meant King Louis did not trust him completely and she would be used as a spy for the King. This was a dangerous position to be in because he was incredibly handsome.

Handsome was not the right word, she corrected herself. Magnificent was the word, with a dignified and chiseled face, a strong jawline and an aristocratic nose followed by two sky blue eyes. His hair was more golden than yellow and his face was tanned so that the eyes popped even more severely against their bronzed backdrop. All of this sat on a well-muscled body that was six inches taller than she was, despite her heels.

Damn the King, she mused. Pushing out her lips in a pout, she knew this man would be a chaotic storm of infinite proportions in her life.

There was no possible way that she would not fall in love with him.

"I can see you are pondering over your good fortune but please, do not bother yourself on my account. I am loyal to the King and only want to reclaim my family's good standing with him. My main concerns are to see all four of my sisters married off to kindhearted gentlemen and to keep my homelands intact. From all accounts, your lands are quite extensive and should join nicely with mine." The sincerity flowing from his eyes was very rare in this pitiless, cutthroat courtly environment, and she could not help but be swallowed up by his sincerity.

Shaking her head again to clear it of how beautiful he was, her mind grasped at one coherent thought of, 'Oh, he also loves his sisters. How kind.'

Hopefully, he was as truthful as he claimed to be because she would hate to report negative affairs about him to the King. However, she did not even know if this was a true account. He could have made this entire scenario up or have false information regarding their match. She would address this with the King.

"Unfortunately, kind sir, I am at a loss in this conversation because it has not been confirmed by the King or anyone close to him for that matter. Although I understand why you would wish to marry me due to my lands and inheritance, I would prefer to hear this from His Majesty."

There, that would gain her some time.

He smiled at Gabrielle with that striking smile again. Yes, he would unquestionably be a dangerous husband who would no doubt cheat on her repeatedly, she mused.

Dangerous to her heart, that is. Everything else about him seemed heartfelt and charming. He most likely needed some direction in his life but besides that, he would be loyal to his family and France.

But it was better to be safe than sorry, she decided.

Attempting to smile in return, she grimaced at him which made him laugh.

"Truly, my lady, you can be quite harsh without even trying. Do you not wish to be married? Has the single lifestyle overtaken your female sensibilities?"

Choking back a growl of anger that came from deep within her, she wondered if he was always just teasing or intentionally trying to goad.

"I will only excuse what you just said because you have four sisters, so surely you try to exasperate all of them with your less than amusing humor, and have now decided that similar behavior bodes well for a future alliance between us as husband and wife."

"Ouch, mademoiselle, you wound me. But as they say, a sharp tongue must be put to use in more ways than one for it to find its true purpose." Quirking up his eyebrows in a comical way, he spread his hands out in surrender.

She laughed. He had somehow managed to make a sexual innuendo about her tongue into a juvenile joke with his hand gesture.

"And finally, she laughs and smiles," he quietly whispered to himself.

But she had very good hearing, unbeknownst to everyone in this place, and she heard him. Had he only been trying to amuse her this entire time? He must genuinely be bored. Or he could be doing this as a wager with others to see who could crack her façade.

Either way, she did not wish to find out.

"Sir, you must pardon me for I no longer wish to be at this gathering. I am tired and the noise is too loud for my taste. I assure you that I will speak with His Majesty regarding this as soon as it can be arranged, and then we can reconvene afterwards to discuss this further," she decreed.

He bowed to her. "As you command, my lady. We will speak soon."

Slightly tipping her head in response to his bow, she realized that he was going to be a gentleman and watch her walk away safely instead of leaving her to watch him walk away from her, as most of the men in this palace did.

It was a pity. Her father would have liked his character; that is if it was truly authentic, she reminded herself. There was no way to be sure of that at this moment.

Walking away while deliberating on the pleasant thought of his smile, Gabrielle was startled to realize that she had made it all the way back to her bedchamber while in this daydream, and her maid was undressing her for bed. The lake would have to wait until tomorrow then.

~~~

The first action she undertook upon waking was sending an urgent note to the King requesting an audience with the line *Surprise de Fiançailles* (Betrothal Surprise) at the bottom to hasten his response.

As her maid finished dressing her in her dark emerald green dress, she was not disappointed when the knock at the door revealed a messenger with a note from King Louis stating he would see her for ten minutes before he took his breakfast.

Following the messenger, she was ushered into the King's bedchamber, where he occasionally met informally with a select few of his court regarding important personal matters.

His manservant was placing finishing touches upon his daily attire.

The King raised an eyebrow upon seeing her but she continued with her curtsy, notwithstanding his seeming annoyance with her.

"Well, well. What have you found out about someone's betrothal? Is it a surprise? Have they gone behind my back and already become married?"

She smiled at him. "Good morning, your majesty. No, my King, nobody has married without your permission. I chanced upon my own betrothal news last night after you had retired for the evening."

The King held a blank expression on his face as he listened to her recount her encounter with her handsome alleged fiancé. She knew he was listening to her but nothing registered on his face. He was a great actor and hid his true feelings from everyone. She was not sure if God himself knew what Louis felt or thought.

Shifting her weight onto her right foot, she awaited his response. He waved his manservant away and turned to fully face her.

"And? What would you think of this happening?"

"Is it true, my King? Have you betrothed me to this man whose father has a sordid reputation in life and death?"

"Are you genuinely asking me this question? Out of all of the people gathered in my court, I had marked you as one who understood the majority of my motives," the King spoke mildly as if talking to an elderly woman.

She paused before replying. Of course, she thought it might have a ring of truth to it but upon hearing no denial from the King, her heart gave a leap of joy. This marriage with a charming man could make her existence a bit less bleak, if he did not break her heart.

"Is he as kind as he seems or is he as money hungry as the rest of them are?" she queried.

"That, my dear, remains to be seen. His sincerity is reported from his staff and close acquaintances, but I always have my doubts about everyone. How could his father be who he was and some of that not rub off on the son? Most sons inherently take after their fathers, especially given time and age. However, it is time that you marry and this is a good match on both sides. Hopefully, he will turn out to be an honest and faithful husband to you and a loyal subject to me. In turn, you will be protected and looked after by a man with four sisters, which means he must be well accustomed to a woman's needs, wants and desires. And this will make up for my misdeed of not letting you return home with your dying father. There is nobody else to look out for you, and thus, I feel compelled to give you an appealing husband," King Louis said thoughtfully.

That was a lovely enough ploy, she thought. If it would appease his pretense of guilt, and he knew she would spy for him, she had no excuse to ask for permission to be set free from the arrangement. Most likely, he would refuse. He wanted her off his 'hands' and into a marriage.

"I am always at your service, your majesty. I appreciate your thoughtfulness in this very personal matter," Gabrielle replied as she curtsied.

He turned away from her and she speedily left the room.

Once out of his chamber, she escaped out the nearest entryway. She needed to think and to be near her mind cleansing water.

~~~

Thankfully, everyone was still indoors having breakfast or getting dressed, although a few people were still in bed. Thus, she had the lake all to herself.

After rowing the tiny boat out a little bit further into the middle of the lake, she reclined back into the bottom of the boat. This was the only place she could take full, deep breaths. Inside that massive, decadent building called 'The Palace of Versailles', she felt trapped and constantly on guard, as if she were a caged bird stared at relentlessly.

Staring up at the sky while her heart slowed down, she allowed herself to release a few tears. Pent up tears from years of frustration, years without her father who was also her friend, years without love and years without hope.

Now it seemed to have happened all of a sudden; a man that she could possibly build a future with and have children with. Even if he might not love her in a romantic way, their children would love her. She would have the love of her offspring to comfort her, and that was a big relief for her.

Her body and soul were tired of being so alone. The last hug she had received was from her maid last month, and that was not the same as a comforting, strong hug from a man.

Thinking upon all of the hugs she would receive from her future husband, she fell asleep with a smile lighting her face as the sun shone down on her, warming her into a pleasurable repose.

~~~

Gabrielle was running through a dark hallway while something cold was surrounding her. The hallway didn't end and she couldn't find her way out. The coldness was covering her entirely, as if a human sized snake had wrapped her up while she slept.

Startled, her eyes fluttered as she woke up and saw the sun was still shining upon her. Why was she so cold?

Upon lifting her arm, she saw the water coming off of her soaked dress as she tried to sit upright. The boat was sinking! It was half full of water!

How had that happened?

She had been so lost in her daydream of her perfect husband that she had not noticed any leaking or hole in the tiny boat.

Trying to stare back at the bank of the lake without causing the boat to sink further, she saw that nobody was about. No gardeners, no hunters, no one walking, nobody.

No, Gabrielle thought. This cannot be happening.

Her dress was completely soaked through and the water continued to rise in the boat.

She screamed, "HELP!" at the top of her lungs and frantically searched for anybody on the grass.

There was nobody.

And she recognized at this juncture that she foolishly could not swim. She had wanted to learn but her father had refused to teach her. He had proclaimed that she would never be alone on water and that a man would save her if problems arose. Now she was caught in the middle of a pond and could not swim to the shore.

She began laughing hysterically.

Where was this savior man now, father?

Panic rose within her. She did not wish to die right now. Her death should at least be in childbirth or something meaningful, not in this pointless way.

This was her own fault. How could she die like this? Alone and with nobody to care.

How deep was this lake? How would she stay afloat? Questions raced through her mind as the panic continued to build.

She did not want to look down but she knew that she only had a few seconds. Her chest was almost covered with water.

If she could undo her dress, it might not drag her completely down to the bottom, her mind racing over all options to keep herself alive.

As she fumbled with her dress under the ever rising water, she damned the person who made all this clothing for women to wear.

Gabrielle could not remove anything other than the top skirt. The corset, the undergarments and the skirts underneath were all tied together.

Dear God!

As she began to flail about, trying to keep herself afloat, she thought she saw someone racing towards the lake. Perhaps it was her future husband! If it was her maid, she was doomed. A man would be needed to pull her to safety under the weight of this dress.

Her head went under and she opened her eyes.

It was very quiet and peaceful under the water. She stopped thrashing and allowed herself to sink.

This was the end and she felt a certain peace and tranquility come over her.

The green-blue of the water was beautiful as the sun continued to light up its depths. Her feet hit the bottom of the boat as it settled against the bottom of the lake.

Trying to bounce off the boat, Gabrielle barely even moved due to the weight of her dress.

'This is it,' she thought. 'God help me,' she prayed as she swallowed water with her last breath.

'Drowning had to be the worst way to die,' a voice in her head whispered. She smiled at that redundant statement as her lungs filled with water and she knew it was the end.

This was not how she had wanted to leave Versailles but in the end, she was finally escaping it.

Her thoughts ceased as she looked up at the sunlight coming through the water and her body felt weightless as she floated at the bottom of the small lake.

Gabrielle sensed a quiet and serene release as her soul left her body.

A few lessons learned in this lifetime:

Nothing is certain in life (sleeping on a boat as she had many times before without incident) so take nothing for granted. Low self-esteem and not believing a man would want her without a king demanding it led to running towards her own death instead of getting to know the man. It is self-sabotage to think that you have all the time in the world to flirt/get married/change your situation; life happens quickly and, if you are not taking control of your life and your reality, can treat you very harshly in order to learn your soul lessons.

Chapter 11

The Afterword

All of these past lives have had an effect on my actions throughout this current life I am living. I had no idea why I had so many issues with my lungs from the time I was born and up to the point that I did past life regressions and trauma release.

When I was born, I had colic, asthma and a list of other things. My mother was in labor with me for three days, and even the final push was a struggle. She did not use any drugs for the pain and was to the point of extreme exhaustion when I decided to show myself.

I was not so much a fussy baby as a sick one. Constantly coughing, never sleeping through the night and upset from lack of sleep, I did not adjust to being in this human form very well. My soul and my human were a bit at odds for the better part of my childhood.

The first issue I had (that I recall) was being unable to breathe. Sitting up in bed during the middle of the night, gasping for breath, I would have asthma attacks. I could feel my lungs squeezing together while no air was entering my windpipe and the terror that would then set in from my human brain screaming, "You're going to die!!!!!!"

And I thought I was dying. I could not understand this as a child – why was I unable to breathe and what triggered this? Was I going to die gasping for air if I could not make it to my inhaler?

When I dug a bit deeper as an adult into these memories of what would bring these attacks on, especially at night, they were due to the beings that would surround me and offer me comfort and other messages. But I didn't know what or who they were (at least my human body/mind/ego did not), my brain rejected what I was seeing, and I would freak out instead of feeling that I was in the company of loving, helpful beings.

Even during the daytime, I would run barefoot in the grass and play with my 'fairy' friends until I was too tired to think. My imaginary world was intense and kept me busy all day long. But - was my imaginary world really imaginary?

There are too many coincidences at this point in my life to know with certainty that the imaginary world of my childhood was simply another dimension which is not visible to the 'rational' human adult most of us become - due to socialization, indoctrination and other means of becoming a contributing member of society that children are forced to learn 'the hard way'.

Around age seven, my mom decided it was enough and cured me of my asthma using herbs. This was very unusual for the 1990's in small town Kansas, USA, and very discouraged by doctors. However, it worked and I didn't look back.

Fast forward to me being seventeen, ready to escape Kansas, and thus, my mom and I took a trip to check out the university that I wished to attend. We decided to visit the Alamo in San Antonio, Texas shortly after the campus tour. If you know anything about what still stands from the original Alamo, it's essentially a wall or two.

I had a meltdown in the Alamo due to a vision of what happened there depicting scenes of blood and gore everywhere: women screaming, men moaning, deafening gun fire coming from somewhere, smoke - I couldn't breathe the smoke was so thick it was choking me. Something was on fire.

Now, this vision could be logically explained as me recreating something I had learned or watched – if I had learned about it. Yes, all Texans learn about the Alamo and how great it was, what it stood for, and blah blah blah, but as a Kansan, there were literally two lines in my history book back in the eighth grade about what the Alamo was, a battle, and how Texas is now a part of the USA.

And if I had seen anything about it on television, which under the scrutiny of my dad was only allowed to show football games, the public broadcasting service (think Little House on the Prairie), or Unsolved Mysteries (which I did not watch because I would get too scared to even go to the bathroom alone).

Basically that two-line history from eighth grade did nothing to prepare me one iota for the death and blood that I witnessed that day walking around the Alamo. Nor did any show that was on PBS or anything aired as a commercial between football games.

So here I am in the middle of the Alamo, witnessing a vision, with no idea that I was not involved in this part of history via a past life, and having a panic attack. My lungs started to constrict as if I was having an asthma attack and I felt as if I were going to die.

It's necessary to state here that I would not comprehend what panic attacks were until I was thirty-one years old, when a doctor explained exactly what they were while I was having one in her office in Midtown New York City.

Needless to say, this was not the first time, or the last time I would have a vision. However, after one momentous vision during my second year of college, I said out loud, "I refuse to have any more of these. I don't want them. I don't know what they are and I'm done with this."

Unknowingly – and also because nobody that I knew among my family, friends or professors could even guide me in this area of visioning – I had just energetically cut off one of my spiritual gifts. And I did not have another vision for ten years after this time.

But this gift would come back after I did additional past life regressions and learned more about my spiritual gifts which can pass from lifetime to lifetime.

~~~

It's all quite fascinating once we start to dig into our own irrational fears, behaviors or patterns that seem to be from outside of our current existence.

When I started living in New York City after college graduation, I had a work hard, play hard mentality. At that time, my mom and step-dad had a timeshare in Cozumel, Mexico, and a group of my girlfriends and I decided it was time to take a break.

We headed on down to Mexico, met up with my parents, and drank our faces off at the unlimited, all-inclusive resort. And one of the girls decided it would be a great time to learn how to scuba dive while we were there.

I enthusiastically agreed to this plan, and we would forgo the drinking in order to do our three dives in three days for our certification. After passing the test we would party, was our thinking.

Part of the reason I really wanted to get certified was because my mother is a certified Master Diver, and her pictures and stories of how peaceful it was underwater captivated me from a young age. The other part was to add another cool, fun thing to my list of 'things I can do on a vacation' – yes, totally my ego and pride.

So there we all were, on our first dive in the ocean (I should add that on our first pool dive we all did great, had fun, it was not that deep, hoorah! We felt ready for the real ocean challenge!), and we needed to buddy up. My best friend and I pair up and, as we start to go under (we are the last ones off the boat), she literally freaks completely out.

"Humans don't belong underwater, what if we die, what if we can't breathe, oh my God! Why are we doing this?!" She's crying with tears streaming down her face as we are floating in the water with the instructor waving us down to follow the rest of our friends into the depths of the ocean.

Then she pulls her mask on, puts her ventilator in her mouth, and proceeds to go down underwater.

I glance wildly around because now my mind is going a hundred miles per hour with, "She's totally right, we don't belong underwater, this is horrible, what am I doing? I don't want to die underwater," and I start to feel panic rising in me.

But I buckle up and say, "I ain't no coward!" and start my descending process, all the while my mind is churning these horrible death thoughts of my lungs exploding during this dive, my instructors not knowing, me getting blood oxygen poisoning, etc.

I should also explain that this was the first time I had truly been underwater in the ocean without my feet touching the sand, and now I had more knowledge crowding my brain as to getting carried off by ocean currents, what we are breathing in the tanks and everything else one learns by reading a scuba diving training manual.

I grew up swimming in lakes and ponds, for heaven's sake! Not oceans where 'Jaws' exists and nobody finds you for days on end, if ever, when you become separated from your dive group.

Needless to say, I hated every second of it. I tried the yoga breathing techniques I knew, I tried meditating, I tried everything to get my mind off of the possibility of dying underwater, but to no avail.

I almost did not finish the remainder of the course but I forced myself to. It was pure torture for my body. I could not breathe correctly for two hours after diving and my lungs – well let's just say it brought up all of the old asthma attack horror to my body and brain.

Once I received my certification (after a deeper dive that again took my lungs a few hours to function normally again, and taking the written test), I decided I would not dive ever again. It was beautiful and peaceful but my body's reaction to it was painful and not worth it, to me.

Almost a decade later, when I was living in Bali, I tried diving again. I thought, how bad could it be and I've most likely outgrown the fear – I didn't even know why I was scared in the first place! I loved the ocean and being underwater – I would hold my breath and free dive to see ruins off of the Balinese coast. Plus, I knew about breathing techniques and taught them as a certified yoga instructor now, so this should be easy.

However, the old fears came back one thousand times stronger as soon as I dipped down below the surface of the ocean, and I could not swim beyond the wading area with the scuba gear on. I went into a full blown panic attack. That was the last time I tried scuba diving.

It was maddening to me that this 'irrational fear' around the ocean and scuba diving was coming up at my older, wiser age. The only problem was that, if I was being honest with myself, this fear had been taking place in lakes and ponds since I was little. I would never stay under water for very long and I would always be within a certain distance from the shore or be able to put my feet down on the bottom of the lake or pond. All of these criteria had to be met or else the panic would start to rise and I would get out immediately.

I laugh now because after one past life regression (the Native American life) with a trained professional followed by a few more on my own, along with the visions from past lifetimes, it's obvious to see it was written all over my soul blueprint. Having drowned, been strangled, shot in the lung and whatnot, the issues with my lungs (asthma, fear of being underwater, fear of drowning, etc.) were very real.

My past lives where this happened could have led to my chronic bronchitis and pneumonia that I had two times a year from ages nineteen to thirty-one. My breathing issues went away as I started to emotionally heal myself, whereas the extreme fear did not go away until my past life regression work.

That is not to say that a person's past lives are the only reason for these deeply held bodily fears and phobias; but it is worth looking into if you happen to have extreme issues which you wish to rid yourself of, especially if you have tried other methods of healing the phobias.

~~~

Equally intriguing is that most of my previous lives were lived in extremes. From one to the next, there was no balance between my relationships or in my working life; I was never happily in love, and I viewed everything in a black and white lens only, which did not allow for the gray areas that naturally occur in any human lifetime.

I was able to see this pattern after writing this book but, thankfully, I had worked on many of these issues beforehand.

I spent most of my teens, twenties and early thirties believing that I could never have everything – a loving relationship, a fulfilling career, my creative side (painting and writing), and a family, simultaneously. I would have to choose between one or the other, which was a long-held belief due to the relationships I grew up around, and only enhanced due to the feminist movement.

'If you wanted to have a successful career, you couldn't juggle a family too,' and vice versa. 'A woman can do everything for herself and by herself. She doesn't need a man, men are accessories.'

Most of the relationships from my childhood were full of people marrying young, infidelity and either ignoring the other person or hating the other person. I saw no people married happily or successfully; marriages were more of a begrudging attachment that was forced by the bounds of the marital institution because divorce was (is) expensive and messy.

Thus, year after year, people stayed married and kept their secrets; the women choosing to focus all of their attention on their children and grandchildren while the men did manly things with their friends, each growing further and further apart, more and more independently of each other with every passing day.

There was a disconnect, to say the least.

I remember thinking at age fourteen that it must be horrible to be married and that true love most likely did not exist, despite all of the Jane Austen novels I had read. I had buried these early examples of marriage into my subconscious, and I did not understand the repercussions of this until my thirties.

Underneath my layer of disgust at these unhappy marriages was a true desire for a committed partner and marriage of growth and love, expansion and traveling, raising a joyful family built on love and trust. 'It must exist!' I would think to myself, having never witnessed it - no matter which friend's parents I visited or any stories I may have heard of throughout the years.

Jumping to the current day, I can look back and see that my subconscious thought of 'marriages all end in divorce or cheating' kept me in a toxic cycle of storming out of bad relationships once there was a red flag that I just could not see past (which there were admittedly many red flags before the dating period was over). Also, due to my past lives, I had lived this division between love life and career repeatedly. It was not only in my subconscious, it was what my soul was used to (and could never seem to rise above) in these past reincarnations.

The majority of my past lives did not look upon sex as a sacred exchange of energy or something done in love, it was merely an animalistic passion/lustful one night stand or a necessary means to an end (begetting children).

I needed to heal the soul loop that I was on in order to grow beyond this limiting belief, and I took the alone time and invested in myself in order to break through the programming of my past; in order to allow my soul to be who I was sent here to be, and that meant being with my true soulmate and co-creating with him.

Presently, I am surrounded by entrepreneurs, writers and artists living their best lives with beautiful partnerships and marriages; couplings that are full of love, support, expansion and trust. I get to witness how these couples show up for each other, weathering difficult times with the belief and faith that good times come after a storm and that there are lessons or growth that is needed when these times occur; that each soul has certain areas to heal as well as experiences to flourish from.

Rather than running away or turning to addiction (of drugs, sex/one night stands, love, alcohol, religion, etc.), they communicate honestly, offer a listening ear, provide space, and 'hunker down' even deeper into their relationship; which brings them even closer and creates more intimacy on a soul level.

After healing myself as much as I could outside of a relationship, I had faith that this would happen for me, that my soulmate relationship would be from and of god (source), and that I would encounter my true partner. And it did happen and here I am, knowing and appreciating everything about our relationship.

I am able to open up my heart further each day to embrace him with every ounce of my being, and this is something that I help other people with as well – this sacred union of two souls, after the nonsense has been removed and the love for oneself is in full swing.

We don't have to choose between this or that; we can have it all, in this lifetime (not some pie in the sky heaven or 'the next time around'). But we must do the necessary inner work on ourselves to make it happen instead of settling for a 'normal' unhappy relationship or an 'expected' white picket fence outcome.

Relationships are magical and full of love, and it is time to bring that belief back.

~~~

There are countless ways to reexamine your past lives. I have experienced a few such as past life regression and hypnotherapy.

If you wish to proceed down that path, finding a trusted and authentic past life regressionist or experienced hypnotherapist is highly recommended. Most will offer an introductory call or meeting in order for you to feel if you connect with them (trust them) or not.

Past lives and reincarnation were not something that I had believed in, based on my very strict Christian upbringing. In college, I stumbled into a religion class and loved it; thus, I became enthralled with the ideas of Buddhism, Hinduism and studying the Gnostic texts left out of the Bible.

There are many authors and teachers who are helpful and each of us must find whoever resonates with us – usually you will feel a prickling along the spine, get goosebumps, feel a blowing of air on the neck, a full body shiver, one of your ears will ring, or the top of your head (your crown chakra) tingles. These types of bodily reactions are a sign that you are heading into the truth for your journey and your soul.

For me, reading books by or watching lectures from Dolores Cannon had a profound effect on my understanding and belief in souls, reincarnation, past lives, etc. Another word for it is transmigration.

Dr. Michael Newton's book, "Destiny of the Souls" on his past life regressions of certain clients, which I read before my own experience, gives more insight into what goes on 'up there' after death. There are many interesting familiarities I felt when reading that book – on a soul level.

Your soul will pull you in the direction you need to go in and towards the book(s) you should investigate. Trust your inner guidance (the loving, soft voice). It will not lead you astray.

~~~

Writing this book gave me a distinct clarity around these distinctive past lives, and helped me illuminate previously unexplainable phenomena from my childhood, tweenhood and adulthood - of this life.

I hope that you can learn from my past-life experiences, maybe something is healed, or that something is sparked within your soul that is true for you which helps you on your journey during this lifetime.

My hope for you is that you take the time to examine your past lives if the opportunity arises and that whatever healing you need or a bit of clarity for your future surfaces, you will wholeheartedly receive what is necessary.

And then you will move onwards and upwards. Joyfully and ardently ready for your next adventure.

Our lives are our own works of art in the format of a movie, and we get to create the script as we see fit and rewrite it as needed.

Knowing and accepting what happened in our past lives, realizing what our soul has carried into this life through our cyclical relationship, health and career patterns, and not allowing those past limitations to hinder us any further – this is how we truly evolve and learn to love ourselves, love others, and continue on our soul mission on this amazing planet during this lifetime.

About the Author

Deeply knowing that she was different from a young age, Acacia has repeatedly taken the road less traveled. Having read all of the books in her grade school library, she tackled high school books and the public library by age 11. Heavily influenced by Hemingway, Fitzgerald, the Bronte's, Bukowski and others, she began writing short stories at age 10 and dreamed of writing a book while sitting barefoot in the tops of trees at her family home in Kansas.

After an 11 year career in NYC, Acacia headed to Bali following a severe burnout that left her questioning why she was on earth. Her winding spiritual path led her back to her writing and oil painting, fluidly combining with years of coaching people and teaching yoga.

She wrote this book in a stream of consciousness and was guided by her intuition at all times regarding every aspect of the book publishing process. Having guided many clients on the journey back to rediscovering their souls and their soulmates via their intuition, she trusted that her intuition was leading her on the right path.

Thus, this lively and intense book was birthed out of her soul journeys. There were other past lives that were not added so that the book remained to-the-point (similar to how Acacia is in real life).

She ardently looks forward to writing more books and is currently working on her crazy autobiography and a children's book along with her artwork. For more information or to contact Acacia, please go to www.byacacia.com.

Printed in Great Britain
by Amazon